PRAISE FOR *Bella's Gift*

"Life takes sudden turns. The horizon brings unexpected storms. The road we walk is prone to go from smooth to rocky in a matter of steps. No one is spared the difficult path. Rick and Karen Santorum weren't. The birth of their daughter Bella was a birth into a life they never asked to enter. Their faith was tested, their futures were rerouted. And, as a result of it all, they are different people. You know the Santorums as public figures in the halls of Congress and on the trails of a presidential campaign. You are about to know them as parents of a special girl. Their struggles, fears, faith, and fortitude—it's all in these pages. I urge you to read this book. Life takes sudden turns for all of us. And we need wisdom from a family who has kept their balance and stayed on the road."

— Max Lucado, pastor and best-
selling author of *Before Amen*

"We love the Santorum family and the way they love children like God loves children. Rick championed the bill to end partial birth abortion in America. The Santorum family has tirelessly fought to return our nation back to the Christian values our country was founded upon. *Bella's Gift* will inspire families and marriages to draw close to God through the joys and the hard times of life."

— Jim Bob and Michelle Duggar,
parents on TLC's *19 Kids &*
Counting

"I have gotten to know Rick, Karen, and their family really, really well over the years. This book is a love story from two parents who walk the walk as husband and wife, father and mother. In typical Santorum style, they pull no punches, but they will also pull at your heart and your soul."

— Sean Hannity, television
and radio host, author, and
political commentator

"One of the joys of being alive is to see love in action and the indelible mark it leaves on the world. Karen and Rick Santorum have written the kind of extraordinary book about their daughter with special needs that moves the heart and stays in the memory."

— Archbishop Charles Chaput

"The radiant truth about special-needs children, such as the Santorums' Bella, is that they give to those around them something that we all need. This gift, that suffuses every page of this marvelous book, is the reminder that every life is sanctified by the capacity to receive and respond to love."

— George F. Will, syndicated columnist

"Bella's father was a Fox News Contributor so I have known about this little child since the day she was born. She is nothing short of amazing—she has beaten all odds! This book is a touching love story about how this very challenged child enriched her family . . . and anyone who meets her. You will be enriched—and inspired—by reading her story."

— Greta Van Susteren, Fox News Channel personality

"*Bella's Gift* is a must read. I've had the privilege of enjoying family dinners at the Santorum's home with the entire family, including Bella. I've witnessed the love that she has for her family and they for her. Bella's story reminds us that love requires sacrifice, an idea that is becoming increasingly lost in our selfish society. Read it. You'll be moved, inspired, and encouraged by the story of this little girl and her heroic family."

— Mark Levin, lawyer, author, and host of *The Mark Levin Show*

"Bella Santorum's story is one that all medical professionals should read and profit from. Her and her family's struggle, besides being inspiring, is also medically enlightening. Too many members of her medical team assumed that her situation was hopeless. This was not so much from a lack of caring as it was a lack of knowing. A detailed, careful reading of the medical literature on children with Trisomy 18 reveals that these children do not have the dismal outcomes that some so-called experts claim. In rare disorders like Bella's, there really are no experts. The ideal professional will yearn to become the expert, seek the truth, know the facts, and assess the entire situation. He or she needs to know in detail all about the child, the medical condition, and the family situation. Only then is one able to really offer good care. Unfortunately, the tendency to 'write off' children like Bella is all too common in modern American medicine with its bottom line, dollars and cents, mentality. Hopefully this book will help to change some of that."

— Michael G. Lamb M.D. and
Kathleen G. Lamb M.D.

Bella's Gift

BELLA'S GIFT

*How One Little Girl Transformed Our
Family and Inspired a Nation*

RICK AND KAREN SANTORUM

with Elizabeth Santorum

NELSON
BOOKS
An Imprint of Thomas Nelson

Published in Nashville, Tennessee, by Nelson Books, an imprint of Thomas Nelson. Nelson Books and Thomas Nelson are registered trademarks of HarperCollins Christian Publishing, Inc.

Thomas Nelson titles may be purchased in bulk for educational, business, fund-raising, or sales promotional use. For information, please e-mail SpecialMarkets@ ThomasNelson.com.

Scripture quotations are taken from REVISED STANDARD VERSION Bible, Catholic Edition. © 1965 and 1966 by the Division of Christian Education of the National Council of the Churches of Christ in the U.S.A. Used by permission.

"Welcome to Holland" ©1987 by Emily Perl Kingsley. All rights reserved. Reprinted by permission of the author.

Interior page design by Walter Petrie.

Photo insert: Photos on opening and closing pages are courtesy "Timeless Portraits by Liz," Sewickley, PA.

Library of Congress Control Number: 2014947431

ISBN 978-0-7180-2195-5

Printed in the United States of America

15 16 17 18 19 RRD 6 5 4 3

To Bella's siblings Elizabeth, John, Daniel, Sarah Maria, Peter, and Patrick: Thank you for making Bella's life so beautiful, joyful, and miraculous. We love you all! Thank you for making our lives complete.

To all the parents raising special-needs children. You are a light in the world and your love inspires us. We pray for you every day.

To Bella's doctors, the ones who never referred to her as having a diagnosis that was "lethal" or "incompatible with life": Thank you for giving her a chance. You are the gold standard for the medical profession.

The LORD is my shepherd, I shall not want;
 he makes me lie down in green pastures.
He leads me beside still waters;
 he restores my soul.
He leads me in paths of righteousness
 for His name's sake.

Even though I walk through the valley of the shadow
 of death,
 I fear no evil;
for thou art with me;
 thy rod and thy staff,
 they comfort me.

Thou preparest a table before me
 in the presence of my enemies;
thou anointest my head with oil,
 my cup overflows.
Surely goodness and mercy shall follow me
 all the days of my life;
And I shall dwell in the house of the LORD
 for ever.

—PSALM 23

CONTENTS

CONTENTS

FOREWORD

Michael W. Smith

Observing a friend or a loved one caring for a special-needs child can be bittersweet. Bitter—because of the pain, stress, and emotional weight they carry; sweet—because of the unconditional love exhibited by families caring for a child who cannot care for himself or herself.

My wife, Debbie, and I have been privileged to view firsthand both aspects of this mystery. We've witnessed the tension, but we have also seen a marvelous example of selfless giving as we have observed Rick and Karen Santorum care for Bella, their *beautiful* child born with Trisomy 18. Most babies born with T-18 do not survive more than a few hours or days. But, despite the doctor's dire predictions that Bella did not have a chance, the Santorums refused to give up on her—and Bella refused to give up on *life!*

I am a fan of the Santorum family. It's not too much to say

that I regard them as heroes. As parents, Debbie and I share similar values with Rick and Karen. We share a sincere desire to instill in our children a foundational faith in God, love of family, and love for our country.

I've known the Santorum family since Rick served with distinction as a US Senator from Pennsylvania. I have appreciated his courageous stands on important issues, but most of all, I have been moved by Rick's love for his family. Our friendship deepened and solidified in October 2006, when I was invited to speak at a memorial service following the tragic shootings at a one-room Amish schoolhouse in West Nickel Mines, Pennsylvania.

Rick was in the middle of his senatorial reelection campaign. He canceled his scheduled rallies and campaign stops to attend the memorial service. Out of respect for the families—and not wanting his presence to have any political overtones—Rick simply sat in the crowd with the other mourners. He supported me that day in a powerful way, for which I will always be grateful.

So when I heard about Bella, I wanted to be there for my friends. I wanted to tell Rick and Karen and the kids that I understood what they were going through, but such words sounded hollow. I'm not sure that anyone can truly understand the overload of emotions that parents of special-needs children experience unless you have been there.

Having a special-needs child is not merely like tending to a child sick with the flu, who, after a few days of rest, medication, and TLC, will feel better. Barring a miracle, Bella's condition will not improve until she gets to heaven. The Santorums know and accept that truth. It would be easy for other family members to become jealous or feel slighted simply because Bella requires so much of Mom and Dad's time and energy. But the entire family pitches in to help. They realize they will be caring for Bella's most basic needs every day of her life, for as long as she lives. Yet they are happy to do so. Rick, Karen, and the kids know that *love* is spelled T-I-M-E.

Every day of Bella's life is a blessing and a challenge for Rick and Karen. Something as simple as going out to dinner, much less dealing with Rick's many responsibilities, requires accommodating Bella's needs. Even getting a sitter for the evening is an adventure, because babysitting Bella is not your average babysitting job.

Yet, I've never heard members of the Santorum family complain of any inconvenience or extra workload they have inherited because of Bella's condition. In fact, if you didn't know about Bella, it is unlikely you would guess the Santorums have a special-needs child. They seem oblivious to anything they might be giving up to serve Bella, what they can't do, or the places they can't go, simply because Bella is unable to join them.

If Bella's needs are great, so is the love she expresses in her own ways. Talk to any of the Santorums, and it won't be long before your hear, "Bella brings such joy to our family." Bella draws them together. Every family member's face lights up at the mere mention of her name. They regard each day with Bella as a gift and they choose to live it in hope. The Santorums are transparently honest and remind us that hope is not a guarantee of satisfaction. It is an inner attitude, a power to believe that life matters. Even if it is not perfect or not what we had expected, it is worth the struggle. They are quick to remind us that the power to embrace and accept life as it is, not simply as we would like it to be, is dispensed from only one Source.

What some people might consider a tragedy, the Santorums have allowed God to turn into a blessing.

In *Bella's Gift*, you will fall in love with the Santorum's special child, but you will also discover the real Rick and Karen Santorum. Within these pages, they reveal their unvarnished innermost thoughts and feelings. They make no attempt to sugarcoat their questions. *Why us? Why this? Why now? Where is God in this situation and how could He allow this calamity to strike our family?* Yet they always come out on the positive side of the ledger, emphasizing, "We receive so much more love from Bella than we could ever give to her."

They share important lessons learned about keeping their own spiritual reserves filled, because the draw upon them is deep and frequent. Perhaps most of all, they remind us what really matters in life.

If you are a person who believes that love is a choice grounded in commitment, yet you wonder at times what that commitment really means, what it asks of you in the hard places, when the arguments for calling it quits seem to be carrying the day, *Bella's Gift* is for you. I must warn you: this book does not pander to wimps. Quite the contrary, the courage and commitment exhibited by the Santorums call each of us to deepen our relationships. They practically dare us to risk taking this journey with them, to risk loving with our whole hearts, to continuously renew the commitments we have made, and to demonstrate our love for one another every day.

Bella's Gift challenges each of us to be less selfish, to give more of ourselves. You may not have a special-needs child, but there is someone close to you who needs some special attention, a special smile, a hug, a pat on the back, or a special word of encouragement. These expressions take little time and don't require a lot of money. Indeed, anyone can choose love over selfishness.

The Santorums effectively remind us that this love requires supernatural assistance—in fact, when you get right down to it, this sort of love comes only from God, working in and through our lives. But that's the good news: His love is enough; His supply is inexhaustible. So when you find yourself growing weary in well-doing, remember Bella's gift to the Santorum family—and to all of us.

INTRODUCTION

• *Elizabeth Santorum* •

I n his letter to the Corinthians, St. Paul told us "now faith, hope, and love abide, these three; and the greatest of these is love" (1 Cor. 13:13 NIV). Love is the greatest of the theological virtues and is at the heart of Christ's teachings. Yet, the dictionary defines love as "an intense feeling of deep affection." If love is merely a feeling, then it cannot be a choice. If the highest similar state is affection, then it requires nothing deeper than tenderness or passion for another.

Love is a concept misunderstood by most of modern society and a look at its origins can clarify what "love as a choice" truly conveys. The ancient Greeks used four words to describe love: *storge*, *philia*, *eros*, and *agape*. *Storge* was familial love and defined the bond man feels toward family, persons, and animals. It often referred to love that is constant, love that one takes for granted. *Philia* described the love of friends or relationships formed based on compatibility and mutual interests. *Eros* was passionate love—not only in a sexual sense, but also in the wonder, appreciation, and desire that man has for sublime beauty.

Finally, the ancient Greeks used *agape* to describe "when one person has much to give to another [who is] more needy."[1] This sort of love exists when there is a generous emptying of oneself in the service of another, without expectation of a reward. It is the love our heavenly Father has for His children.

When my sister Bella was born, I was a seventeen-year-old girl without a proper understanding of *agape* love or its practice. No doubt I received plenty of that deepest form of love from my parents growing up, but I had taken its existence for granted. I loved my parents and my siblings in the sense of *storge* and *philia*, but did not distinguish it from my other pleasant, reciprocal relationships. My ambiguous conceptions of love encompassed everything without noting any distinctions. My shallow understanding of love was challenged and deepened when Bella was born and diagnosed with Trisomy 18. I assumed that my little sister would never be able to love me in a way that was familiar to me. We would never share clothes, talk about her crushes, or paint each other's nails. I only saw dependency, not reciprocity.

I wanted to love her, but I did not know how. Honestly, I wanted her to be able to love me too. I was blind, selfish, and afraid. Yet, when I held Bella for the first time, I saw her fragility and, with it, her perfection. I saw her vulnerability, not her helplessness. She was not passive but responded to me in ways that showed an open receptivity to my love in the form of simple, newborn appreciation. As I watched her, another Bible verse came to my mind, "My grace is sufficient for you, for my power is made perfect in weakness" (2 Cor. 12:9 NIV). God would do mighty things through this little one. Her vulnerability was the perfect vessel to manifest His strength.

As I held her, I saw that her perfect vulnerability would require a more perfect, *agape*, love. Bella's very life demanded it. I initially feared this dependency, partially out of selfishness and partially out of unfamiliarity. As I stood next to her at her baptism several days later, I promised to be her godmother, to instruct her and guide her on her journey with Christ. Yet, it struck me that I would learn more about God from my meek, dependent, and "disabled" little sister than I could ever hope to teach her.

She called me to practice *agape* love. I would be called to imitate the love of our Lord for me, to truly walk with Him day by day in my journey with Bella. I could ask nothing in return from her, except for the love that she gives me every day. I am continuously humbled by the example of my parents as they selflessly and joyfully care for her, in both good days and bad. To them the radiance of their beloved baby girl is a reward in itself.

Bella has taught me there are different kinds of love and that the highest form of love is self-giving and chooses the beloved even when it proves difficult. The way our family lives has changed dramatically in the past several years and we wouldn't have it any other way. Bella is at the heart of our home, a quiet and smiling reminder that every day is a gift. Her tenacity, strength, and unqualified love encourage us daily. We have learned that life is not centered on our individual needs; it is about living for Christ and serving others with a Christlike *agape* love. Love is not about what we can gain; it is about what we can give.

In the following pages, my parents share the story of Bella's life from their distinct perspectives. They grieved in different ways, but they grieved together. When the realities of caring for a special-needs child could have driven them apart, they held each other even closer. When Bella reached milestones and celebrated huge victories, they thanked God for them and shared in the joy of her life.

As I write this, Bella sits here with her hands on top of mine. Occasionally, she'll look up at me, find my face with her hand, and then return to following my hands on the keyboard. She reminds me of how we all must look to God the Father, we who are so in need of His love and reassurance. May Bella's story witness to the transforming love that these special children bring into a world that so desperately needs to experience the self-giving love the Father has for His children.

1

LOVE IS A LEAP OF FAITH

• *Karen Santorum* •

*I consider that the sufferings of this present
time are not worth comparing with the
glory that is to be revealed to us.*

—ROMANS 8:18

There were five. Five fragile, tiny fingers held the cord that monitored her heart. The lifeline was coated in grey rubber and connected to a machine. Up. Then down. Then up. Then down. The jagged line stenciled her vitality. Glass separated me from her, her beautiful heart that I longed to

1

know, to comfort. I put my fingers to the glass. There they were, those five perfectly formed fingers. Did they reveal that much? I saw nothing lacking. I saw her vulnerable figure, her soft skin, and her wisp of curly hair. Like mine. Her hair was like mine. Three pounds, fifteen ounces of body and soul grew to visible perfection in the safety of my womb.

Sometimes I still can imagine Bella kicking within me. All the more reason why every feeling revolts at seeing her outside of me, before it was time, before she was strong. Did I fail to protect her? She shifted in the isolette, hand releasing the grey line. I saw it then. To this day, I wish I had imagined it, that there was a mistake. Pinkie finger and index finger rested on top of the two middle fingers, points touching. There was my sign. That natural and simple movement had shattered my hope, because my sweet little girl had just displayed one of the classic markers for Trisomy 18.

The doctors had tried to prepare me. As Bella grew in me, they knew that something was "off," but without prenatal testing, they were unable to determine exactly what. A rare genetic disorder called Trisomy 18 was only one of the possible diagnoses. *But no, not that,* I had thought. I was so sure. So sure.

We had given away our baby things and thought we were moving into the next phase of life, but God had other plans and blessed my womb once more with another child. Surely He would protect her. But doctors had done tests, confirming what I had never dreamed possible. As a nurse, I knew what this meant. Of the 10 percent of babies with Trisomy 18 who survive birth, 90 percent don't make it to their first birthday. The prognosis was terrifyingly bleak; the odds were stacked against her. My little girl, my Bella, had an extra eighteenth chromosome in every cell of her body, making a genetic code doctors call "incompatible with life." Lungs shutting down, holes in her heart, kidney problems, and severe intellectual disability were horrors we should expect.

Like the blood pounding in my head, the list of symptoms boomed like a frosted iron hammer pummeling my heart. Yet, for some reason, I needed to see for myself. I had to look at my darling little girl and see some physical manifestation of the fatal condition she was dealt. Her delicate hands, those five fingers: they were my sign that she did in fact have Trisomy 18.

Within those whitewashed halls, I had no concept of time. It passed like water running through my fingers. My husband, Rick, and I were ghosts in a hollow world that was frozen inside hospital windows. Cheap blinds provided a thin veil between the fragility of the ill and the vivacity of the healthy world. Stooped shoulders, cold acidic coffee, rubbing alcohol, dripping IVs, beeping monitors, and white walls defined my physical reality.

A haze had come over me, my eyes never free of tears. I had so many questions and no answers to satisfy the screaming voice in my head that asked, *why?* My child had been given a death sentence. Scrubbed doctors with words of compassion that felt hollow and insincere told us mere days remained until her body would fail her. No surgery could fix this, no medicine heal it.

Fruit baskets and flowers filled my hospital room as I recovered from the C-section. Rick and I were supposed to be receiving congratulatory cards celebrating the birth of a new life. Instead, paper notes with cheap expressions of sympathy mocked me from my bedside table. Did they make cards for "staying alive," not just "getting well"? And then there was the silence from those who did not even acknowledge Bella's life. It was as if she did not exist. They appeared to ignore everything that made my Isabella Maria unique and wonderful.

My heart was angry and bitter, lashing out in response to such acute sorrow. When my other children were born, we were overflowing with joy and left the hospital within twenty-four hours. Would my new little one know nothing but this sterile cage? Hurt and anger burned through me, searing hot in my veins. I felt heat and, with it, some sense of life again. How can life and death be dealt in the same hand, at the same moment?

My hands rested on my stomach, feeling the stitches from the C-section. The first I'd ever had. Five fingers skimmed the coarse line that held my incision together. I winced in discomfort as I flexed my stomach muscles. The pain was horrible at first, but not now. There was an ache, a dull ache. This six-inch stitched line was a tangible representation of those scars left on my heart by a different kind of scalpel. Time would heal the gash in my tissue, but at that moment I doubted that even eternity could heal the gash in my heart.

Rick was a strong husband through this dark time, but I didn't know how he could be at peace as a father. As always, he took things standing up. He brought me coffee, food, clothes, and comfort. He took off work, cared for the other children, and held me as we both cried. He told me we were going to get through this together—with emphasis on the word *together*. I can still see Rick sleeping on the hospital room sofa with a couple of the children, while a few of them were in bed with me. We were completely exhausted.

On Sunday, five days after Bella's birth and the day after we had received the diagnosis, we walked to the coffee shop on the ground floor of the hospital. I took my coffee black that day. I never used to enjoy the hot bitterness without milk, but now I felt that it made me stronger. I couldn't really taste it anyway. Rick's brown eyes were soft, searching my face. I suppose my expression was vacant, my blue eyes listless and out of focus.

"I wish they would at least let me see her face. It's hard enough that she can't nurse," I whispered. The doctors had Bella on a CPAP machine to help with her breathing and kept a mask over her eyes for the first few days to prevent optometric damage caused by the lights. Like other babies with her condition, she was fed through a feeding tube, as she lacked the ability to nurse.

Rick held my hand. "Soon you'll know her eyes."

I knew God had a purpose for Bella's life, but this did not lessen the pain of my broken heart. "When am I going to see her eyes, Rick? When they don't have life in them anymore? Tell me! Aren't you angry?" My voice was strained and coarse. I didn't really want a response to the question, as I knew we were in two different places. Even in those days, Rick was at peace with God, with His plan for our little girl. I could not boast the same confidence. God help me, I could find no goodness or purpose in Bella's diagnosis.

Rick's eyes looked away from mine and then down as he said in a whispered voice, "I'm at peace with everything." Hearing him say that made me feel so confused and upset.

I wondered how Rick could be "at peace" during such a painful time. Peace is not something you feel when a doctor gives your daughter a death sentence. Peace is not something you feel when your life is, in an instant, changed forever. Peace is not something you feel when your daughter is in the neonatal intensive care unit. Peace is not something you feel when you've been abandoned and thrown to the far corner of a desert. Peace is for the *next* phase, maybe in a year or two, after going through the fire and clearing the rubble. At a time like this, peace is simply the last thing a parent will feel. I moved my cup of coffee away and got up from the table, weeping and barely able to stand from the pain of the surgery, and said what I sometimes say to my children, "I love you so much, Rick, but I really don't like how you're acting right now. I just don't understand." We walked back to the neonatal intensive care unit (NICU) together, but I felt alone, as an unbearable loneliness seemed to suffocate me.

◆   ◆   ◆

The children met their sister, Isabella Maria, for the first time on the day she was born. We decided to call her Bella because it means "beautiful," and she is beautiful. All of them came in to see her: Elizabeth, John, Daniel, Sarah Maria, Peter, and Patrick. We were trying to fit a lifetime of love into what we were told would be a short life.

As they entered my room, I hugged them all so tightly, so desperately. My shoulders shook with silent sobs. Their hearts were heavy, and they needed to be assured that Bella was going to be all right. "Mommy, you look so tired. Are you okay?" My six-year-old, Patrick, knew that something was wrong, but not exactly what that meant. He squirmed away from my embrace, looking at me with innocent concern and confusion in his wide, brown eyes.

"Mommy's getting better, sweetheart. I'm so happy to see you."

He smiled in self-assured contentment. Peter and Sarah quickly curled up under my arms, buried their faces in me, and cried.

Rick and I did our best to explain to our children that Bella was going to be all right. We needed to protect their delicate hearts and minds and assure them that we were going to get through this together as a family, that we were going to love Bella and care for her just as we cared for them, and that if she left us, she would be with our Father in heaven, knowing only love. We framed everything in the light of faith and described the legion of angels who might come and take Bella to heaven. We also described the NICU world in words and pictures and told them that everything in and around Bella was there to help her.

Patrick proceeded to buzz to the nurse's station, telling them he had a new baby sister. The other children wandered over to the NICU window, elbowing for the best view of Bella's isolette. I looked at Rick as I struggled to stand up. His eyebrows furrowed in concern, hands flexing as he deliberated whether or not to help me up. We had not spoken since yesterday. Then, Rick took both my hands, then wrapped his arms around me, and said, "This has been the hardest thing I've gone through in my life. I want you to know that. I'm just trying to understand it as best as I know how. What I do know is that *Bella is who she is, and we're going to love her just the way she is.* I think it's wonderful that all she'll ever know is love. Our love." And we stood there together, eyes united.

◆   ◆   ◆

"Mom, look: I got a green one! And green's my favorite!" Patrick held out a sticky lollipop he had received from the nurses. Somehow it had already found its way onto his shirt and face.

Peter whipped around upon hearing that: "Patrick! Blue is better than green!" Peter, our eight-year-old, has always argued with Patrick about which color is better.

Kids. Rick and I smiled. It felt good. We all cleaned our hands and put on scrubs. Patrick didn't even protest when the nurse took his green lollipop. Could they all sense how important this moment was? Rick and I helped the children into clean hospital gowns that were far too big for them. Hospital policy only allowed one of the children to visit Bella's isolette at a time.

We decided that Sarah, who was ten, would go in first. She had prayed for a little sister for so long and understood the seriousness of her condition, but perhaps not the severity. Holding Sarah's hands, Rick and I walked with her into the NICU. Sarah bent down so she was eye level with Bella. Silence at first. Mouth formed in a wondering *o*. Eyes taking in everything in front of them. She looked up at me, then Rick. Receiving our smiles and nods in return, she turned back to look at her new baby sister. Brushing her hair out of her face, she leaned in closer, nose nearly touching the glass, and then sat in the rocking chair next to Bella's isolette.

The nurse carefully placed Bella into Sarah's arms. She had removed the eye mask, but Bella's eyes remained tightly closed against the harsh hospital lights. What came next was barely audible, a timid whisper. "Hi. I'm Sarah, your sister. I prayed to Jesus that your angel would have a pink ribbon. Mom said that would mean you were a girl. I've always wanted a baby sister!

My whole life!" Sarah paused. Looking up at me, she smiled. "Mom, she's like my baby doll! She's so small." Beaming with pride and joy, she looked back at Bella. Sarah's smile disappeared as the beeping of the heart monitor startled her. The beeps stopped, and Bella's heart rate went back to normal. Staring intensely, Sarah said, "Oh my gosh, you're so cute. I'm sorry you're sick. I'm praying for you, Bella." She kissed her as she said, "I love you, Bella."

Outside, the world kept turning, everyone moving in his or her own direction. I now realize most people scatter in times of true suffering, overwhelmed and awkward when words fail them as they attempt to console. They're right. Often, words are not enough. But I will never forget those who were there to sit with me, cry with me, and share the silence. Yes, words can be inadequate, but I think it's worse not to try. My dear parents and family called me every day, offering support and consolation. My mother's compassionate heart and unwavering inner strength anchored me during that stormy time. I vividly remember my sister Kathy saying, "Karen, of all the members of our family, you are the one who can handle this. Your faith will get you through." I didn't believe her.

My friend Susie visited me when others shrank away. I'm grateful for that. She brought me flowers that added some warmth to the cold room. She was wearing khaki capri pants and a linen blouse; her brown hair was pushed back behind her ears. What a pair we must have made, me with my hospital gown, raccoon eyes, and unkempt curls thrown up in a desperate bun. I'll never forget Susie's face during that talk. It was warm. Her smile was soft and understanding, even through tears. She brought light and warmth.

We sat together, I tried to describe what I was going through, and she patiently listened. She knew. She knew the immense heartache. We talked about faith and the need to trust completely in the will of God. My faith, which had previously been a consolation during challenging times, now offered little comfort. I was mired in tormenting questions. I wanted to know why God would have done this, why He would have allowed this. I wanted to know how God, the God I had loved so completely, could be so unloving and so distant. I felt abandoned. It seemed as though my pleas for help were not heard. It felt as if I had been thrown into the desert.

As a Christian, I knew the symbolism of the desert, but now I experienced the reality: the aridity and deep sense of loss and loneliness. During those long, lonely nights in the NICU, I thought about Jesus and about Moses, Abraham, John the Baptist, and so many others whose faith was tested in the desert. The desert meant long periods of silence and fasting and enduring the enemy's attacks. I didn't understand what was happening. My time in the hospital and wrestling with the diagnosis was a desert time.

My friend Susie offered the hope and comfort of an oasis during that desert time. Susie came into the NICU every day. She took pictures, organized meals at our church, helped with the children, drove our pastor Fr. Alexander Drummond, in for Bella's NICU Sacrament of Holy Baptism and Confirmation, and held me together. "A faithful friend is a sturdy shelter: he that has found one has found a treasure."[1] Susie was and is a treasure.

Bella's baptism was a significant moment in her life and in ours. Rick, me, Elizabeth, John, Daniel, Sarah Maria, Peter, and Patrick were all in our hospital gowns gathered around Bella's isolette. Elizabeth was Bella's godmother, and our dear friend Mark Rodgers was her godfather. They are two very holy people in the spiritual care of an angel from heaven. Heavy hearted and exhausted, we stood and prayed as Father Drummond led us in prayers for our Isabella. He placed a white garment over Bella symbolizing her purity as she "put on Christ" (Gal. 3:27). Father then anointed her head with oil as a reminder that Bella was receiving the Holy Spirit. Since we were in the NICU, we could not light the candle, but it was there to remind us that Bella would always be a light to others. As he poured the water over Bella's head, he said, "[I baptize you] in the name of the Father and of the Son and of the Holy Spirit" (Matt. 28:19).

This moment always filled Rick and me with so much joy as we welcomed our infants into the Church and promised before God to raise our sons or daughters in the faith. At the moment of our children's baptisms, we were on a lifelong mission to pray that our newly baptized baby would live a life that was pleasing to God and guided by the teachings of Christ. Bella's baptism was different. Something so holy was taking place and all the focus was on Bella, but it was somber and there were a lot of tears. None of us even noticed the bright lights or heard any of the NICU alarms. Rick and I just kept hugging the children and telling them that we loved them. Susie was there taking pictures and capturing moments that in our exhaustion we do not even remember.

Right after Bella's baptism, Father Drummond looked at Rick and me and asked what confirmation name we would like to give Bella. Rick and I were surprised, because we did not know that Bella was also being confirmed. We looked at each other and at the children and laughed for a moment since confirmation names in our family usually took months to decide. Everyone agreed that Bella's confirmation name should be "Fátima," after Our Lady of Fátima, since she was born on her feast day. So Isabella Maria Fátima is her name, and the circle of grace that was given to her just moments before at her baptism was completed with her confirmation (Acts 2:1–12). There was no party that followed, only quiet reflection on the significance of what had just happened. Our Bella was now part of the body of Christ; part of our church family.

◆   ◆   ◆

Rick and I were constantly in the NICU, keeping our vigil at Bella's isolette. During Bella's ten-day stay in the NICU, we all held her, sang to her, and rocked her. We were trying to fit a lifetime of love into what we were told would be a brief life. The care was excellent, and the physicians and nurses were kind and compassionate. That is, except for one doctor.

"You must be her parents." The physician extended his hand. "I'm one of the attending doctors for the NICU. I am so sorry for your . . . situation." We shook his hand in turn. His skin was tan, his smile white. He was about fifty, with an overbearing presence, and his cologne was out of place in the sterile room. He, like other doctors and medical literature, described Bella as having a "lethal diagnosis" and referred to it as "incompatible with life." The stark utterance clanged like a hammer against an empty cistern. Rick looked at me and squeezed my hand.

I turned to the doctor, "Thanks for your concern, Doctor, but we'll continue to fight for Bella's life. She's clearly exceeding medical expectations."

The doctor looked mystified. "I don't know why you would want to do anything. You have to let her go. Statistically, there's no hope here." He walked away, not knowing he had prodded a momma grizzly by talking about my little girl like that. My claws were out. *She is not a statistic. She is not a diagnosis. She is my child.* The medical community is filled with many like him who weigh the value of life according to IQ or in terms of one's usefulness. They were not going to dismiss my little girl so easily.

◆　　◆　　◆

One week had gone by since Bella's birth. Seven days more than the skeptical and scientific said she would live. One hundred and sixty-eight hours of life, unexplained and miraculous. I remember sitting at Bella's isolette when the "why do anything?" doctor came over. My eyes flashed and my primal instinct kicked in: the momma bear stood between this scavenger, not healer, and my baby. It did not matter to him that Bella was stable and doing much better than expected. He was rude and had about as much warmth as a lizard. Dr. Iceman. He did not refer to Bella by name and kept telling me not to look at the monitor. My gaze turned stony when he pursed his lips and said, "Well, I think it's best if you don't grow attached to *the baby*. It's for the best."

I froze. Shocked. How could he imagine that I had not loved my little girl from the moment she was in my womb? I love her with a love infinite and unqualified, a mother's love. My voice quaking with emotion, I responded, "I *am* attached to *Bella*. In fact, I've been completely in love with her since knowing of her existence, and *that is what's best.*"

◆　　◆　　◆

During this time our babysitter, Bridget, was a lifesaver. She took great care of the children and kept our home running smoothly. It was a comfort to know that our children were being well taken care of in my absence and with such a kind, holy, and virtuous woman whom they had known for several years and who was like a big sister to them. My oldest children helped with meals and in a hundred different other ways every day. They were in school and visited Bella when they were able to. We thought that keeping their lives as normal as possible with their schoolwork, sports, friends, and music lessons would be best for them.

After a long week in the NICU, Rick and I continued to spend hours holding each other and staying with Bella. Garbed in a polyester hospital gown, I shuffled to the NICU sink to wash my hands for the hundredth time. As on all previous nights, I traced my fingers along the glass wall that kept me from her. We kept a prayer vigil at her isolette, a special bassinet used for infants who are born prematurely. It provides a controlled temperature, proper humidity, and openings for tubing from IVs or oxygen. But most important, we provided what no machine can and what every child truly needs and deserves: love.

Rick was asleep in the rocking chair next to Bella's isolette. Did I look as tired as he did? How I love that man. Darkness inhabited the room, save for the steady glow of red and green numbers on the monitors. Blood oxygen saturation: 98 percent. Heart rate: 147 BPM.

The night nurse interrupted the silence. "She's doing fine

tonight, darlin'," she said. Wearing Winnie the Pooh scrubs, she was an older, maternal-looking woman with rich, almond eyes.

"She is, isn't she?" I returned, managing a shadow of a smile.

"You know, she never cries. Always peaceful-like. Talking to the angels, I suppose. Do you call her Isabella?" the nurse queried.

I hesitated. Saying her name always brought tears to my eyes. "Isabella. Isabella Maria. That's her name, but we call her Bella." I choked.

The nurse's face lit up, and she smiled. "Bella. Now, that fits. I know that means 'beautiful' in Italian! Beautiful."

"Yes. She is that." I smiled at her more fully this time. "Thank you." I paused and continued watching my sweet Bella. "You know, I love her like I've known her forever. Time doesn't really count when you're talking about love. I want to tell her that, to look into her eyes. I bet they're beautiful too."

Walking over to stand at the isolette with me, the nurse gazed at Bella, who was waking up. It was almost dawn now, the beginning of her eighth day of life.

Turning toward me, the nurse said softly, "Would you like to hold your baby girl, your Bella?" She didn't need to hear an answer. I looked at her, though I thought her words too good to be true. Every chance we had to hold Bella was a great gift and blessing. The whole family held her every day despite all the tubes and wires, and every day I tried to nurse her. Tears filled my eyes as I nodded. I was going to hold my Bella again; that basic maternal instinct would be satisfied once more. I woke Rick. He was groggy but didn't want to miss any moment when we had the chance to hold Bella. The nurse opened the door on the side of the isolette. After fiddling with the probes and wires, she bundled Bella and took off her eye mask.

Bella opened her eyes. They were a beautiful blue and fringed with long, dark lashes. Angel eyes. My breath caught in my chest as I beheld them. Those piercing blue spheres locked with my own. I was utterly captivated, breathless. Lifting her from the bed, the nurse placed her into my arms. My left hand cradled her while my right reached to touch her face, her hands. She was so light, her skin pink and soft. Nose like a dewdrop, and dark hair that was fine, silky, and curly. Flush cheeks with rosy little lips. She was like a porcelain doll.

I held her left hand with one of my fingers. Those five beautifully formed fingers grabbed mine so tightly. When her fingers were holding mine, she didn't hold them in the way that had identified her condition. Together, we were whole. I drank in every detail of her. Her gaze was mixed with love and a sense of knowing. *Thank you for loving me. I love you.* Hot tears rolled down my face, tears of joy. Her eyes searched me, focusing on my face as I leaned in closer to her. Bella's right hand reached upward, though not sporadically, as is typical for an infant. I lowered my head, and her hand touched my cheek. My breath caught in my throat. Tearful laughter. I closed my eyes as I felt her warm little hand on my skin.

I suddenly realized Rick had been holding me, his steady hands supporting me in these fragile moments. I opened my eyes and whispered, "I love you, Bella. I love you." I don't know how many times I repeated those words or how long we sat there. Together, we were suspended in time. I never wanted those moments to end.

In all those precious moments with my little girl, something changed in my heart. I experienced the joy and the love that she brought to us, and that tuned out the improbable statistics. I focused on the gift of my baby girl and the hope for her life. Clarity came when I saw those blue eyes. Soon, we would learn the impact of the gift we had received; soon, Bella would come home.

●　　◆　　●

As we were preparing for Bella's discharge, I noticed we were being sent home without a prescription for oxygen, even though Bella needed it with her feedings. Unfortunately, Dr. Iceman was the doctor in the NICU at that time. Approaching him, I asked if we could please have a prescription for oxygen so Bella could get through her feedings.

"I just don't think it's necessary. You have to learn to let go."

My fists clenched as I exhaled. Being able to feed our baby was undoubtedly "necessary."

Rick took a big breath as if he were going to scream and slowly said, "All we're asking for is oxygen."

I went on to say, "Doctor, I'm happy to talk to the other doctors in the NICU or the hospital management, because we both know Bella needs oxygen when she's trying to nurse. We're not leaving here without a prescription for oxygen."

Eyebrows arched, he pursed his lips as he reached for his prescription pad.

During our last day in the NICU, Bella's geneticist, Dr. Ken Rosenbaum, talked to us once again about the devastating statistics pertaining to Trisomy 18 infants. My heart heavy and cold, I heard but hardly listened anymore. I'd heard the bleak statistics. Again. And again. Then he surprised me: "There is hope."

Hope. I raised my eyes and felt something different from cold numbness or hot anger. He smiled softly at my reaction, leaned forward in his chair, and told us what we desperately needed to hear: "Bella will write her own book, and I hope it's a good one."

2

LOVE
NECESSITATES
TRUST

• *Rick Santorum* •

Cast all your anxieties on him, for he cares about you.

—1 PETER 5:7

I stood just off the stage at the Republican National
Convention. I was about to walk out to speak to thousands
in the arena in Tampa, Florida, and millions around the country, and all I could think about were her hands. I closed my
eyes and I saw them, so soft and dainty as I stood next to Bella

in the isolette in the neonatal intensive care unit the day she was born. I had stood not only as a father soaking in a precious moment with our beautiful little girl, but also as a detective looking for evidence. There had to be some clues. The doctors had been sure for months something was wrong, but they couldn't identify it.

The daydream was abruptly broken with the words: "Ladies and gentlemen, former senator from Pennsylvania, Rick Santorum." That was my cue.

The main theme of the speech was restoring the American dream. I concluded by reflecting on my interaction with Americans during the course of my 2012 presidential campaign.

As my family and I crisscrossed America, something became so obvious to us. America is still the greatest country in the world—and with God's help and good leadership, we can restore the American dream. Why? I held its hand. I shook the hand of the American dream. And it has a strong grip. I shook hands of farmers and ranchers who made America the breadbasket of the world. Hands weathered and worn. And proud of it. I grasped dirty hands with scars that come from years of labor in the oil and gas fields, mines, and mills. I held the hands that power and build America and are stewards of the abundant resources that God has given us.

I gripped hands that work in restaurants and hotels, in hospitals, banks, and grocery stores. Hands that serve and care for all of us. I clasped hands of men and women in uniform and their families. Hands that sacrifice and risk all to protect and keep us free. And hands that pray for their safe return home. I held hands that are in want. Hands looking for the dignity of a good job, hands growing weary of not finding one but refusing to give up hope.

And finally, I cradled the little, broken hands of the disabled. Hands that struggle and bring pain, hands that ennoble us and bring great joy. They came to see us—oh did they come—when they found out Karen and I were blessed with caring for someone very special, too, our Bella. Four and a half years ago, I stood over a hospital isolette staring at the tiny hands of our newborn daughter, whom we hoped was perfectly healthy. But Bella's hands were just a little different—and I knew different wasn't good news. The doctors later told us Bella was incompatible with life and to prepare to let go. They said, even if she did survive, her disabilities would be so severe that Bella would not have a life worth living. We didn't let go, and today Bella is full of life and she has made our lives and countless others' much more worth living.[1]

That speech was given after four years of wonder, delight, trial, and anxiety—four years of living with and caring for an oh-so-fragile living miracle. But when I stood next to her in the NICU shortly after she was born, I had a different set of experiences to draw upon that shaped my understanding of the situation. This was not our first rodeo. Karen and I had already ridden this bull, been launched into the air, then trampled on the ground, and it had left its mark on us.

Almost twelve years before, I had stood next to Karen at a hospital in Pittsburgh, awaiting the birth of our fourth child. This was nothing, however, like the three previous births. The little boy on his way into the world was not ready to be born. He was just past the halfway point of developing in Karen's womb, and we knew his lungs were not mature enough to survive long. Yet that was his fate, and we were powerless to save him.

The saga had begun a couple of weeks before his birth as I stood next to Karen in another medical facility, as the sonographer was going back and forth with her wand over Karen's abdomen. Karen and I had brought our three children—Elizabeth, John, and Daniel—to see the newest member of our family. It was a routine twenty-week exam, and we were excited to learn whether we were having a boy or a girl. The kids had their preferences, but the standard answer for us was "happy and healthy!"

I noticed the sonographer was looking at one particular area over and over again, so I asked if there was a problem. Her response was less than reassuring. "The doctor will review the results with you when I'm done," she said.

A few anxious minutes after she left the room, the doctor returned, and, with a few words like "Let's see what is going on here," he moved the wand around to that same area. Again we asked whether there was a problem. After a few moments, he turned to us and said, "Your son has a fatal birth defect and is going to die."

So much for bedside manner.

Through all the emotions that spilled out during the next twenty-four hours, we focused on two things. First, giving him a name. We weren't about to let doctors, our friends, and prayer partners refer to him impersonally as "Baby Santorum." Our child was not going to be an "it" or just a "son"; he was every bit a part of our family as were the other children. His name would be Gabriel Michael, after the two archangels.

Second, we were determined to do everything possible to give him a chance to survive outside of the womb. Karen and I fought side by side, talking to every possible doctor and specialist to find somebody, somewhere, who could waken us from our nightmare and treat our son's condition. We ended up in Philadelphia, under the care of a brilliant and exceptionally skilled surgeon, Dr. Scott Adzick, where Karen and Gabriel underwent intrauterine surgery to save his life.

Miraculously, it worked! The doctor said that although Gabriel was not out of the woods by any means, he should have a good chance to survive the pregnancy. He also said that, as with all surgeries, complications could occur. He focused on the one they always warn you about when you have surgery—infection. His orders were quite emphatic: "If Karen's temperature starts to rise, go immediately to the closest hospital."

We went on with life, believing we had dodged the bullet, that our fight had given us a much-deserved victory. The very next day we headed to Pittsburgh for Karen's parents' fiftieth anniversary party. The following day I was in the car, heading to Erie on Senate business, when my mobile rang. It was my sister-in-law, Nancy Garver. With her voice cracking with emotion, she said, "Rick, turn around. You need to get home; Karen has a high fever. I am so sorry. I am so sorry."

We all knew what that meant. The womb keeping Gabriel alive was dying. The surgery had caused an infection in Karen's womb, and the infection would kill her if it weren't treated. When we arrived at the hospital, Karen was already in labor, her body doing what it had to do to survive. The physicians in Pittsburgh confirmed what we were told in Philadelphia: the only way to stop the infection from killing Karen was to let nature take its course and deliver little Gabriel. He was not even twenty-one weeks, and even without all his complications, we both knew that delivery meant death for our son.

It was the worst night of my life, trying to comfort my dear Karen, delirious with pain, while she pleaded with me not to allow Gabriel to die, to let him be born. Our dear friend Monsignor Bill Kerr, at the time the president of La Roche College in suburban Pittsburgh, was at Karen's bedside through the night, comforting us. As the night went on and Karen's fever subsided, we were able to convince her that she was doing all God would ask her to do—to be the best mother she could be for as long as she could.

Shortly after midnight, the monsignor took leave, but left us with holy water to baptize our little Gabriel in the unlikely event he would survive this horrible ordeal.

In the wee hours of October 11, 1996, he surprised us all. The doctor delivered him and, with an air of disbelief in his voice, he pronounced Gabriel alive. Praise God! We knew he was a fighter to have survived his condition, then surgery, but to endure labor and delivery at his age was a miracle. Through tears of joy and sadness came the faint words "Baptize him." Karen held him in her arms as I poured the water on his forehead, baptizing him in the name of the Father and the Son and the Holy Spirit.

The nurses wrapped him in a baby blanket and left us alone. There was nothing they could do, so they let us spend a lifetime with him, his lifetime.

For the next two hours, Karen and I held Gabriel, took pictures of him and us, and told him how much we loved him over and over and over again. I never took my eyes off of him—I was afraid I would forget what he looked like, so I wanted to engrave his face in my memory forever. We sang to him, prayed to God, and as his heart, which we could see beating in his tiny chest, began to slow down, we thanked him for fighting the good fight. We thanked God for giving us those moments to meet him, hold him, love him, and pray with him. When his brave little heart stopped beating, for a moment ours did too.

It wasn't until after the funeral that I began to deal with the reality of life after Gabriel. More than any other emotion, I felt betrayed, by God. You see, after many years of faith not being an important part of my life, the previous two years had been a time of spiritual renewal for Karen and me. When I was elected to the Senate, we moved our family to Northern Virginia and attended a church where the pastor, Fr. Jerome Fasano, was different from the "meat and potatoes" priests we were used to. He lit a fire in us at the very same time we encountered another great man of God, the chaplain of the US Senate, Lloyd John Ogilvie. My faith went from something I did on Sunday to being at the heart of my life both at home and at work.

I rededicated myself to my family, who had played second fiddle to my run for the Senate, and found a passion for the most vulnerable in public policy. I put political considerations aside and weighed in on the most controversial issue of the day, abortion, when I led the fight on the floor of the Senate to ban partial-birth abortion.

After chasing my desires, I began to pursue God's will—and now this was His response? I recalled a quote from Saint Teresa of Avila, who, after experiencing numerous trials, complained to Jesus. He responded, "Teresa, that's how I treat my friends."

Teresa responded, "No wonder you have so few friends."

"Ask for the gift of understanding." These were the words of Chaplain Ogilvie that I held on to during this time. "Please, Lord, just make sense of all this," was my constant plea. He did not disappoint.

In time, I was able to see God's love through the pain. Now, as I reflect on the night that encompassed Gabriel's life, I am comforted that in that short life my son knew only love. How many can say that? God's gift of faith reassures me further with the belief that Gabriel is now with our Father in heaven. The thoughts of a life knowing only love and an eternity nestled in our Lord's bosom lifted the weight of grief over time. It also made me realize my most important role as a father is to shepherd my children to our Father in heaven, because, in the end, all that really matters is the end.

This realization helped me trust that He is a loving and just God, who loves my son even more than I do, but I still missed Gabriel, missed holding him, caring for him, and watching him become an honorable man. I couldn't see that God was at work, primarily through Karen, to lift Gabriel up to touch, heal, and even open the eyes of those who would not see.

Gabriel's life is chronicled in Karen's book *Letters to Gabriel*, as well as in the media reports and interviews that followed its publication. The book was published in 1997, but there isn't a month that goes by when someone doesn't come up to me to thank us for writing the book and telling our story. Even in our darkest moments, God is faithful. I have often said to my children, "If you can accomplish for our Lord what your brother Gabriel inspired with his life, you will be a great warrior for Christ."

My experience with Gabriel taught me to try and live, not as the world tells me to, in the here and now, but in the here and there, as well as the now and then. Gabriel's death helped me live fully in the moment, but with my mind's eye focused on the eternal—trusting in God to help me navigate through the shoals.

♦   ♦   ♦

Bella was small for her age, so late in pregnancy we were referred to a perinatologist, a specialist in dealing with high-risk pregnancies. At our ages, Karen and I were the definition of high risk. A battery of tests showed just enough to keep us on edge, but not enough to have us really worried—suspicions, but nothing definitive. After Gabriel, the hope for "happy and healthy" had become the hope simply for "alive," and we would fight it out from there.

As all three-plus pounds of Bella were fighting for her life and she was hooked up to so many contraptions that you could only see her hands, I was praying one prayer: "Not again, Lord, please, not again." But her hands told a different story. Her pinkie and index fingers were ever so slightly curved in toward each other. That was it—a marker for Trisomy 18. Of all the possible conditions, this was the one the doctors were most concerned about, so this was the one we researched the most intently.

Statistics. I didn't like them when I earned my MBA at Pitt. I've seen them twisted for political advantage and used to validate lies, but I hated this one the most. Of all Trisomy 18 children diagnosed in the womb, 90 percent don't survive birth, and of the 10 percent that survive, 90 percent don't live to see their first birthdays. This condition had a 1 percent survival rate. I was never a dad who pushed his kids to be a 1 percenter—you know, the top 1 percent of income earners that the radical left likes to rail against—but I had always believed they were capable of reaching whatever goal they set their minds to. Now I looked at that 1 percent as the equivalent of climbing Mount Everest.

How would I handle telling Karen and the kids what I had discovered? *Should I even tell them? If I don't, how should I prepare them*? How can anyone be prepared to hear that the child you think is perfect is going to die, and soon? Most T18 children die within the first few weeks after birth.

I could have been wrong, so I contacted the pediatrician and told him of my discovery. His response was the predictable: "Let's wait until we get the test back. No use speculating when we will know for sure in a few days." Of course, he was right, so I decided to take the same approach with Karen and the kids. No use jumping the gun, particularly when, in spite of all the evidence, Karen was holding firmly to the hope that Bella was going to be okay. But I also was determined to do my best to begin to lay the groundwork for what was likely to come.

Karen and I both were voraciously reading as much information as we could on T18 to find some light in the impending darkness. The more we read, the more hopeless it seemed. As I prayed about how to handle this, I just kept coming back to my experience with Gabriel—when I'd learn to trust in God and believe, as the great hymn says, it is well with my soul. In fact, I don't recall ever being so alive in the Spirit as I was during those few days. I realized that was the only way I could hold my family and myself together as the waves were about to crash down.

When the day came to receive the test results, I was convinced Bella had T18. But that was only part of the story. I had learned that, as with almost every condition, there are degrees or ranges of severity. In the case of Trisomy 18, there was "full" and "partial." Children with partial T18, while still severely challenged, have fewer physical and mental issues and thus have a much better chance of survival. We had spoken with the geneticist, and he was optimistic that if she did have T18, it would be the less serious, mosaic condition.

That was our prayer, and Karen's heart was holding on to hope. Bella was sailing along, even though she weighed less than four pounds, was five weeks premature, and was unable to eat much by mouth. Even for a normal baby she was thriving, much less for a baby with a fatal condition. In Karen's heart the indicators were a variation of the norm and nothing more; Bella was going to surprise everyone and either not have T18 or have mosaic T18.

In the days while waiting for the test results, we read all we could find about this condition. Karen's father had been a brilliant medical geneticist, so this was very much in her wheelhouse. She knew the gravity of the diagnosis and was hoping and praying for a miracle.

"I am sorry, but Bella has full Trisomy 18." The doctor's words ripped like a bullet into our hearts.

"Are you sure it is full . . . full Trisomy 18?" I asked.

While the doctor provided what seemed to be a million caveats, the answer came back to me as yes. Our little Bella was going to die.

Even though I'd suspected the worst, I didn't really have time to digest it all. Karen needed me. I had to comfort and encourage, even when there didn't seem to be any hope. The coming to terms with it came later, when I had to inform our family and friends that, in spite of their prayers, another child was going to be taken from us. We just didn't know when or how. The calls were cathartic, even though I had to explain the details over and over again, but my sole focus was to love and serve my family. Someone had to rise above and hold us together.

What helped me the most during this time was my faith and the thought of my son Gabriel. I thought of the horror of losing him and yet the blessing he still is to our family and me, and the impact his life has had on others.

◆　　◆　　◆

Of the 10 percent of T18 kids who survive birth, a very high percentage die in the first few weeks, and the doctors were sending Bella home on hospice care. We had to fight for appropriate life-sustaining care while accepting that she would not live long. I decided to deal with that reality by accepting and being at peace with God's will for Bella.

I had some tough moments, but I was the rock for the family. Sometimes too much so. Karen would get upset that I wasn't going through the pain and anxiety in the same way she was. I learned quickly that explaining how I was holding it together was not a good idea. My task was to affirm her way of dealing with the grief, while also loving her and helping her recover.

After ten days in the NICU, Bella was on her way home. It was a joyful and anxious day. It had been six years since we had a baby and we had thought we were out of the baby business, so we had given away all our baby stuff. In spite of the diagnosis, we decided to proceed with setting up a cute nursery. We had a bassinet set up for her, but Karen insisted on buying a crib for the day when Bella outgrew the bassinet.

Ever the practical guy, I wasn't always sensitive to the emotions in the house. Like the day Elizabeth and I were unpacking the crib. I told her to save the box that Bella's crib mattress had come in. She looked at me, confused, and asked why.

"Well, we just don't know how long Bella is going to be here."

I wish I could take those words back, because I'll never forget the way she looked at me, as though I had not only hurt her but condemned Bella myself. My feisty Lizzie grabbed the box and tore it up as she started to cry. "You have to believe in her!" she said. "You have to have faith! If you don't, then who will?"

Looking at the pile of cardboard, I felt ashamed. I hugged her and we both cried. I knew she was right, but I just didn't know how I was going to believe that Bella could survive when it seemed so impossible. Losing Gabriel taught me to trust God's will, that all will be well in the end. Elizabeth reminded me that accepting God's will didn't mean abandoning hope.

3

LOVE THROUGH PAIN

• Karen Santorum •

*It takes courage to love, but pain through love is
the purifying fire which those who love generously
know. We all know people who are so much afraid
of pain that they shut themselves up like clams in
a shell and, giving out nothing, receive nothing and
therefore shrink until life is a mere living death.*

—ELEANOR ROOSEVELT

We Love Bella's Dad"
Written in silver glitter ink on a piece of pink
poster board, the words waved back and forth in a sea of

enthusiastic supporters. My husband and I were walking down the rope line, shaking hands and being photographed. After being on a presidential campaign for several months, we'd seen our fair share of campaign literature, T-shirts, and even some eclectic, homemade signs during the many rallies we had held. But this was new. Cameras flashed, reporters hounded us with questions, and smiling faces encouraged us. Yet in that moment, everything slowed as I looked beyond the fray.

"We Love Bella's Dad"

A plethora of pretty, red-crayoned hearts framed the words. I craned my neck to find its artist in the crowd. Then, as her dad lifted her above the crowd and onto his shoulders, I saw her: blonde pigtails tied up with ribbons, blue eyes, and a sincere smile. She had Down syndrome. Walking over to them, excitement evident on my face, I introduced myself and thanked them for coming. The little girl's name was Julia. She was there with her parents and her big brother, Michael. Complimenting them on their artwork, I asked who made the sign.

Michael, who was no more than eight, replied quickly and enthusiastically, "Julia did the hearts, but I did the letters, because I'm her brother and I'm a big helper." The little guy's cheeks were red as he bashfully twirled the rope line after his proud declaration. Smiling, I told Michael that he must be a very good big brother. He beamed in response.

Julia waved the sign back and forth as her father lifted her from his shoulders and set her on the ground. Looking up at me, she bashfully tilted her head and smiled. I bent down. "Hello, Julia. I like your sign."

Her smile turned into a grin as she looked at it herself and said, "It's pink and so pretty!"

It was.

"I love it, Julia! Do you know pink is Bella's favorite color too?"

Surprised and excited, Julia said, "Wow! Give her a kiss from me!"

I smiled and opened my arms as she came to give me a hug. In a sea of people, during long days of traveling and campaigning, this moment renewed my sense of purpose and determination.

Turning to their mother, I was moved by the reaction on her face. Smiles and tears simultaneously crossed her countenance. Reaching for my hand, she whispered, "Thank you for giving us hope."

I squeezed her hand, smiling as a silent moment of understanding passed between us. I knew the fears, struggles, and joys of a mother with a special-needs child. I was one of them.

◆   ◆   ◆

January 28, 2012. This date is seared in my memory as one of my most difficult days as a mother. On that day, the story of my youngest daughter's disabilities came into the spotlight under complicated circumstances. Several days after the South Carolina Republican presidential primary, our sweet little Bella got very sick. We had taken our entire family down to South Carolina before the primary to campaign. During our trip, Bella had enjoyed many walks on the beach and the healing sea air. Then, the day before we left to go home, she began to get sick. What was initially a runny nose went into her lungs. Pneumonia. She was lethargic and out of sorts. My first thought was to get her home, back to her comfort zone. I had been a neonatal intensive care nurse for years, a background that was invaluable in a moment like this.

Rick continued on to Florida to campaign for the next primary. As he hit the trail, voters clamored for all the candidates to release their tax returns. Unlike the other candidates, Rick did our taxes himself, your average-Joe Quicken user. So, he had to return home to compile them for release.

Back at home, we hoped Bella would mend quickly and not get worse. After trying every measure and treatment to help her turn the corner at home, I was at a loss to help my little girl. No color in her face. Breathing labored. As she let out a cry that turned into a cough, her heart rate soared even higher. It had been increasing since we'd returned home. Her lungs were filling. She had to get to the hospital. Providentially, Rick's twelve hours at home to get our tax records came right in time for him to rush her to the hospital with me.

Admitted to the pediatric intensive care unit (PICU), Bella was stabilized by the medical staff. They attached tubes, probes, and wires. I watched, silently. I've done what those nurses were doing. I've put in more IVs than I can count and hooked up vital monitors, which means I know when they're doing it right, and frankly, when they're not. Those nurses did their jobs quickly and correctly.

Bella was in critical condition: pneumonia in both lungs. Rick and I were exhausted and worried sick. If she kept declining, we would have to put her on a ventilator, a dramatic step that we did not want to take.

Rick quickly decided he couldn't leave with Bella in intensive care. We then faced a difficult choice: whether or not to release a statement about Bella's hospitalization. We understood that if Rick left the campaign trail with no explanation, the news networks would speculate that he was a lazy campaigner, or worse, leaving the race. With the Florida primary just days away and three more primaries within the coming weeks, there was a lot at stake. All of this, however, was peripheral to our main focus: getting Bella through this crisis.

Nonetheless, a decision had to be made. If we released a statement about Bella's hospitalization, we risked intrusive reporters infringing on her privacy and the talking heads debating as to whether or not this was simply a shrewd political move. In moments like this, I once again turn into a momma bear with her claws out. I am fiercely protective of all my children, but particularly of Bella. Filled with fear and trepidation, I was not about to relinquish my little girl's privacy only to have the world pick her apart. Rick's perspective was very different from mine. By doing a press release, he hoped the world would see Bella as we do: as a beautiful gift from God. Her life would be a witness in and of itself, and maybe, just maybe, people would begin to pray for her.

Rick's staff laid the decision squarely on our shoulders. They shied away from any political talk, offering prayers and support. Rick and I went back and forth about the possible outcomes. What if people found out what hospital she was in? Would they try to catch a glimpse of her as fodder for the nightly news? A million thoughts ran through my head. I didn't want to put her in the line of fire. But what if people did pray for her? We talked to a dear friend about the decision.

He reminded us, "God gave you the gift of Bella, but her story is not your own." He was right. After praying together, we decided to introduce the world to our little girl.

The press release went out. We took a leap of faith that God would protect Bella and our family. Sitting in the tiny hospital room, Rick and I kept watch at her bedside that afternoon. As I read our drowsy little girl *The Runaway Bunny*, I glanced at Rick, who had fallen asleep sitting up in a chair. He deserved some shuteye. I don't know if he'd truly gotten a good night's sleep in the past year.

Sure enough, he was awakened a few minutes later by the buzz of his phone that never seemed to stop. New e-mail. New phone call. New text message. New news. New challenges. New victories. He started to respond and looked at me, bleary-eyed, then put his phone and tablet on the table. He came and sat next to me. We finished reading the book to her together, drowning out the sound of beeping monitors and buzzing phones.

As the day went on, the response to the news that Bella was in the hospital overwhelmed us. Our in-boxes were flooded with notes of encouragement, prayer, and support. The witness of a three-year-old little girl moved people in all walks of life from around the country. We got notes from people who didn't agree with Rick politically that said, "Thank you for being a voice for the special-needs community" and "I really admire you for taking time away from the campaign trail to be with your little girl."

Bella did something in the midst of a heated primary season that no one had been able to do until this point: she refocused our family and many others on what was really important. For the first time, there was unity between the campaign camps as people prayed for Bella. Rick received thoughtful notes from many of the other candidates who were offering prayers for our little one.

Suddenly, Bella was headline news. Featured in major papers and on the largest networks nationwide, our three-year-old was a subject of national interest. For the most part, the dialogue was positive. People talked about her tenderly, even sweetly. I admit that I was happily surprised. I hadn't known what to expect. I had feared they wouldn't see her the same way we did, that they would see her as broken or sickly. She is neither. Bella is a joyful gift, a sweet little girl who gives nothing but love.

Commentators started discussing important issues surrounding the special-needs world, such as the legal struggles that occur when special-needs children aren't given fair medical treatment, or any treatment at all. A whole host of issues were brought to the forefront of the debate, dealing with families, the pro-life movement, the special-needs community, and so much more. It was as though people realized the pro-life movement doesn't end at birth, but it continues at the bedsides of the disabled, the elderly, and the vulnerable. Bella put a face on the helpless, those whom society looks upon as "useless." Ironically, these children give perfectly the most important thing of all: *love.*

◆　　◆　　◆

Like so many times before, we took turns staying with Bella and spending time with the other kids at home. She was never alone. As we watched over her, we witnessed something miraculous.

Within twenty-four hours of the press releases going out, Bella turned the corner. She went from critical condition, almost ready for a ventilator, to being clearly on the way to healing. Rick and I firmly believe in the power of prayer. As I watched Bella smile again, her overnight transformation witnessed to the belief that prayer can do improbable, if not impossible, things.

We ultimately decided to continue in the campaign for the same reasons we had decided to get into the race in the first place. The motivating force was the future of our children, especially Bella, in the wake of the Affordable Care Act and its effects on our nation and, in particular, children with disabilities.

People all over the country fell in love with our little girl, and from then on, "How is Bella?" was the main question everywhere we went. We carried pictures of her to show when someone asked about her.

As folks started to learn more about Bella, we discovered that more and more people were bringing their special-needs kids, like Julia, to our campaign events. We even met several beautiful children with Trisomy 18. The parents of these children talked to us about their struggles, and all were different, but a common thread ran through their experiences: the irreplaceable joy and love their mentally or physically challenged children brought to their lives.

During the past few years, many people have encouraged us to tell Bella's story, to write about her. The problem was we did not know where to begin or what to say. Bella is only a little girl. In the eyes of the world, she is not particularly successful or accomplished. On the other hand, she is larger than life, and her few years have allowed her to impact the lives of many.

Our frustration was not tied to a constricting word count, but rather to the boundaries of language.

Words don't do justice to her sea-blue eyes, her smile that overwhelms your heart, or her giggles that have all of us in stitches. Language has its limitations. With that in mind, we hope to share the story of a little girl who has never lived according to her limitations, but rather by the boundless nature of her spirit.

4

LOVE ENGAGES
THE WILL

· *Rick Santorum* ·

As in water face answers to face,
so the mind of man reflects the man.

—PROVERBS 27:19

Being pro-life can mean different things to different people. Living pro-life is a definitive walk. Gabriel and Bella transformed a policy position of defending the unborn to a passionate battle for the dignity of every human life.

Contrary to the media characterization of pro-life politicians being driven by their religious beliefs, I decided to defend human life from conception until natural death through science. Like most Americans growing up in the sixties and seventies, I didn't give abortion much thought. It had not touched my life or my friends or family, so I was never confronted with the choice. If the topic ever came up in conversation, I steadfastly took an accommodating stance.

That was possible, even in political circles, thirty years ago. I had been in politics since my college days and had even worked for a state senator, Doyle Corman, who was a pro-choice Republican from central Pennsylvania. Senator Corman and his wife, Becky, are like second parents to me. And their son, Jake, who replaced his father in the state senate, is like my little brother. During the entire time I worked for Senator Corman in the early 1980s, I don't recall a single serious conversation about the abortion issue, probably because in those days it was easy to steer clear of "those" types of issues.

That noncommittal stance served me well until after a few years of practicing law. I had this ridiculous idea at age thirty to run for the United States Congress in suburban Pittsburgh. To my surprise, I started to get questions about my position on abortion. In the first few exchanges with voters, I practiced the chameleon approach. Unfortunately, this multiple-choice position on abortion soon proved untenable—who knew? This was a serious and increasingly important public policy issue, and I needed to give it the same rigorous analysis as taxes or foreign policy.

At that time I was a churchgoer, but more of a punch-your-time-card-on-Sunday kind of Catholic. I knew my church's position on the issue, but that wasn't going to be the deciding factor. I treated abortion like every other issue; I wanted to get all the facts before making my own decision. As a lawyer, I had read *Roe v. Wade* and thought I had a handle on the law. The Supreme Court in 1973 stated that they couldn't determine when life began, so they ruled that a fetus doesn't have any rights during the first three months of pregnancy. After that, the fetus acquired some rights in the second trimester and even more in the final trimester. If the science backed this understanding of the nature of the human fetus, that biologically and even metaphysically the fetus is not fully human, then I would be on board with the court. If not, then it all depended on where the science led.

I discussed my conundrum with my then girlfriend, now wife. It so happened that her father, Dr. Ken Garver, was a world-renowned specialist in medical genetics. He was also a great defender of children with Trisomy 21 and wrote extensively about the dangers of eugenics. Who better to ask the facts about the science of when human life begins? (It was also a great way to make a good impression on my future father-in-law.)

My position on abortion would boil down to two points— one legal, one medical. The legal issue was straightforward. The Fourteenth Amendment to the Constitution states, "nor shall any State deprive any *person* of life, liberty, or property, without due process of law." The Amendment doesn't define *person*, but it does define *citizen* as "all persons born and naturalized in the United States." So the unborn are not citizens, but are they *persons*, and therefore entitled to protection from laws that legalize abortion?

Who qualifies as a person? Webster defines *person* as "a human being." So at what point does humanity begin? I wanted

Dr. Garver to help me answer the question: At what point do those cells in a mother's womb become a "human being"?

After dinner Karen's dad walked me though the scientific literature to explain not only when life begins but also the scientific consensus on this point. He was such a bright and caring person, and he spoke in a way that was understandable to someone without a medical degree. Here is the long and short, in layman's terms, of my lesson that night: A zygote is created at fertilization, or conception. A zygote has the complete complement of unique human genetic material, thus at that point it is human. A human zygote can't develop into a kangaroo or a mouse; it is human.

Is it alive? Webster defines *life* as "an entity that metabolizes, or converts fuel into energy." Dr. Garver pointed out that from the moment of conception, the zygote begins to metabolize. In other words, the zygote is genetically human and alive and, therefore, a human life or person. I love my father-in-law for many reasons and will always be grateful to him for guiding me on so many important issues.

From that night forward, I knew I had to be pro-life. Years later—in fact, right after the 2012 campaign—a television host in California introduced me to his audience by stating, "The Senator believes life begins at conception—"

I interrupted him immediately and emphatically said, "No, I don't!" The host froze right on national TV.

"You don't?"

"No," I said. "I *know* life begins at conception." I wasn't going to let this reporter put my pro-life position in the realm of faith or belief. I came to my decision based on science and 4D ultrasounds that allow us to look with stunning detail at the baby in the womb and reinforce what science confirms.

Why isn't everyone pro-life? I know many otherwise wonderful people who elevate personal autonomy over the rights of "a group of cells that don't look like a cute little baby." But even most who hold that opinion also oppose abortions when the fetus begins to look more like a baby.

Gabriel and Bella were both candidates for abortion. Both infants' obstetricians felt compelled to advise us that the most popular *option* for parents carrying children like Gabriel and Bella was termination—in other words, abortion. In a world that values abilities, either physical or mental, a child that is *dis*abled is less valued, particularly in the womb. I witnessed this debate firsthand before either Gabriel or Bella were born.

When I came to the United States Senate, I had a 100 percent pro-life voting record in my four years in Congress, but I never took to the floor to debate the issue. In fact, I had made up my mind that I would never cross that red line in politics where I would be marginalized as a pro-life zealot. In all likelihood, one or two speeches on abortion would not draw the wrath of the abortion-supporting media and interest groups, but coming from a lean Democratic state like Pennsylvania, why risk it?

That was the game plan, but in my first year in the Senate, I went through a spiritual transformation. I often say I came to the Senate and found the Lord! Many people think He has long abandoned that place, but in fact, I found many people of faith not only in the Senate but also in ministries devoted to helping people working in the Capitol.

It just so happened that this spiritual transformation was occurring at the time the Partial-Birth Abortion Ban Act was being debated in Congress. This bill sought to ban an abortion procedure performed on babies that were at least twenty weeks old. I was appalled to learn it was legal for a twenty-week-old fetus to be deliberately delivered alive in a breech position, then killed by the doctor as he or she held the baby and thrust pointed scissors into the base of the baby's skull. I was shocked even more by watching senators defend this horrific procedure. I could no longer stay silent. I decided to rise and speak against the gruesome practice.

When I went to the Senate floor to speak, you would have thought I had never spoken in public in my life. I was done before I realized what I had said, which turned out to be little more than gibberish. Thankfully, my staff kindly cleaned up my remarks in the *Congressional Record* so they could make some sense. Nine months later, due to a variety of circumstances, including my finding faith, I was on the Senate floor again talking about the issue, only this time I was leading the debate. I was now managing the override of President Clinton's veto.

The debate was as intense as a debate over life and death should be. Even though I was trained as a lawyer, I had done very little criminal work other than an internship at a public defender's office during law school. During that debate, I felt I had to bring the passion of a defense attorney who was trying to save an innocent client from being executed. But it wasn't just one, but hundreds of victims, who would die a brutal death if I failed.

Even though I was in my first session as a senator, it was not my first time around the block. I had managed the welfare reform bill earlier that summer to successful passage, so I was ready for action. But this was a battle beyond the object of the legislation. This was the ultimate moral and spiritual battle playing out on an unlikely stage. As a thirty-eight-year-old first-term senator talking publicly about this grave issue for the first time, I should have felt chastened or even over-whelmed. I didn't. Thanks to prayers of support, I had never felt more in the zone.

President Clinton had vetoed a few bills from the Republican Congress, including welfare, but this was the first congressional attempt to override a veto. That was front-page news in every paper in America. As expected, the House had easily overridden his veto, so all the coverage was on the debate in the Senate, where the result was uncertain. This debate was not just about the bill at hand, but the coverage was going to shape public opinion in advance of an election and provide the arguments for candidates running against opponents of the ban in key Senate races around the country. The debate on the Senate floor really mattered.

In the closing hours of the debate, I was struck by the defense mounted by the pro-abortion senators. Senator Dianne Feinstein from California succinctly advanced their argument: "Some women carry fetuses with severe birth defects late into pregnancy without knowing it. For example, fetal deformities that are not easy to spot early on in the pregnancy include: cases where the brain forms outside the skull, or the stomach and intestines form outside the body, or do not form at all; or fetuses with no ears, mouths, legs, or kidneys."

She and other senators were using examples of children with disabilities (some with problems that are treatable) to jus-tify their opposition, suggesting that the government should not stand in the way of parents who want to kill their chil-dren once they find out their babies aren't perfect. While this stance came as a shock to me, particularly from some senators who had taken the lead in advancing the cause of the disabled, in retrospect it shouldn't have. I knew that a very high percentage of parents who find out about disabilities through prenatal testing abort those babies. Some studies have put the abortion rate in such cases as high as 90 percent.

Let's set aside the fact for now that, according to doctors who performed this procedure, 99 percent of these abortions were performed on healthy babies; let's wrap our minds around the idea that dozens of US senators, including, later on, Hillary Clinton, opposed the partial-birth abortion bill because it protected disabled children from death.

I don't recall any of these senators during the course of six debates over eight years ever citing the case of a healthy baby to rationalize their opposition. This bias drove me to respond: "Think about the message we are sending to the less-than-perfect children of America and the mothers who are right now dealing with the possibility of delivering an abnormal baby. My wife is due in March. We haven't had a sonogram done. We are hopeful that everything is fine. What message are you sending to me in looking at that sonogram in a week or two, if the doctor says to us that our child isn't what we want?"

Even though we lost the fight, I felt certain I was following God's will. I was devoting more time at home to Karen and our three little ones, and my prayer life was better than ever. Less than a week later, Karen, the kids, and I walked into that sonographer's office, and that doctor, in fact, did tell us that Gabriel was going to die.

I had followed what I thought was God's will to defend the lives of these little babies from a horrible death, *and He kicks me in the head*? My son's condition could have been an example used by Senator Feinstein as a reason to abort. I was now forced to decide whether I was going to be true to my words, which had been so easy to speak on the Senate floor. Was Gabriel indeed no different from any of our other children?

I felt God was putting me to the test. After going through a period of vacillating between disbelief, anger, and a resolve to fight, I had an epiphany. It struck me what an amazing opportunity God had given us. It was no coincidence that I had led the debate on partial-birth abortion a week before this sonogram. It was no coincidence that children with disabilities were being used to justify that procedure. And it was no coincidence that I had mentioned our soon-to-be-born baby as an example of accepting all God's children into our human family, no matter what their condition.

I thought maybe this wasn't a test at all but the perfect opportunity for God to show the way. He was going to use Gabriel's condition as a sign for the world that He loved every baby in the womb. I was convinced God was going to save Gabriel's life so I could tell the miracle of His love not just for the unborn but also for the disabled.

We were encouraged that the doctors could surgically fix Gabriel's condition in the womb. They cautioned, however, that, should Gabriel survive in the womb long enough to be born, they weren't sure he could survive outside the womb. And if he did, he would have serious health issues involving constant care, expense, and stress. I was ready for a miracle, but was I ready for all that Gabriel's life could bring?

Frankly, I never faced that possibility in my mind. I was convinced Gabriel was going to be the miracle boy. I could see

God's hand everywhere in this saga. He was not going to pass up the chance to let the world know of His glory!

I dove into my plan for God's glory, but there was no water in that pool. Gabriel died, and with him, my plan for revealing God's glory.

As God revealed His plan through Karen's book *Letters to Gabriel*, I saw how faithful He had been in the end. I also saw how living through this pain of having a baby in the womb with a severe problem gave me a powerful personal witness to share. The abortion debate was now very personal. It spurred both a passion and compassion. Passion to defend what I now knew firsthand—that child in the womb is one of us, part of our human family—and compassion to help all the wounded women with unplanned pregnancies who had believed the lie of sexual freedom without consequence.

I championed every pro-life bill in the Senate for the next twelve years, including the passage of the Unborn Victims of Violence Act and the Born-Alive Infant Protection Act. I fought for funding for pregnancy care centers that provide care and support for pregnant women in a crisis situation.

To me the pro-life debate was about abortion first and foremost. Then Bella arrived on the scene to teach me a whole new dimension of the issue.

◆　　◆　　◆

As I previously mentioned, I was horrified that senators wanted to keep late-term abortions legal so parents could kill their children if they found out they were disabled. As the lead sponsor of the bill, I was bombarded by letters from parents of disabled babies in the womb who were outraged because they had to go to multiple hospitals to find both an obstetrician and a hospital willing to deliver their babies. Most reported that the hospitals were more than willing to do an abortion but didn't want to risk the legal liability of delivering a child with severe health complications.

As we became more involved with the pro-life issues, we discovered the battle is also waged at the bedsides of the very sick and disabled. It is one thing to know of parents fighting to get care for their babies or trying to find professionals to deliver their babies; it is another to be a father afraid to leave his child's side for fear of what may happen when he is away.

George W. Bush made the case for education reform with a devastating line that put the educational establishment on its heels. He referred to the lax attitude and standards of education professionals for minority and poor children as the soft bigotry of low expectations. When it comes to medical professionals and children in the womb with severe mental or physical disabilities, the soft bigotry of low expectations for the disabled is often deadly.

The culture of death is everywhere. Not that the hospitals are crawling with evil mercy killers, but rather, with many people who value human life according to what a person is able to *do*, rather than on how he or she can love and be loved. Bella, like so many other people with severe disabilities, can't "do," but she is loved, and we are especially blessed that she can love. What is more valuable than that?

5

LOVE THROUGH
CHANGES

• *Karen Santorum* •

One sees great things from the valley;
only small things from the peak.

—G. K. CHESTERTON

Ten days after she was born, Bella came home from the
hospital. Outside the hospital walls, the sun was shining. The weather seemed to be God's way of welcoming us
home. I'll never forget fitting Bella's tiny body into her car
seat. She seemed lost in the infant seat, with her curly-haired
head nestled in the preemie head support. Looking at her

bewildered expression and wide eyes, Rick and I smiled. As she tried to stretch but couldn't seem to move in her little coat, we laughed for the first time since her birth. It felt good to hope. Our little girl was coming home. She had graduated from the NICU. She had survived the combat zone when no one thought she would. No one except us.

Although usually a lead foot in the car, Rick drove slowly. Coasting over the bumps, he took care to make sure Bella wouldn't wake up. As I watched scenes of office buildings change to trees and sky, I exhaled. I inhaled. The May air was fresh, not sterile or tinged with rubbing alcohol. I heard the hum of the engine and the silence of my own thoughts. Spring was changing to summer. Closing my eyes, with the sun warming my face through the window, I felt like a bird just out of a cage. Fresh air and sunshine were the perfect medicines to begin healing my brokenness.

When we arrived home, we heard pounding footsteps from upstairs and squeals of joy. "She's home!" All the children were there to welcome their sister. As they rushed into the hallway, they beheld her. Their animated excitement turned quickly into hushed, awe-filled whispers. The little boys started tiptoeing closer, eyes wide with anticipation. Gathering around her, they were all mesmerized.

Bella had fallen asleep in the car but had begun to shift and awaken to the sound of their voices. A pink hat hid her curly hair, and her rosy skin lay against the soft, downy blankets surrounding her. Such serenity. We watched as her long eyelashes batted awake, revealing her sea-blue eyes that moved to take in all the faces surrounding her. Sarah reached and grabbed Elizabeth's hand. Caught up in the moment, I felt a knot forming in my throat and then Rick's arm around me. Strength returned to my limbs.

Above the doorway to our family room, our children had hung a huge, colorful birthday sign, lovingly decorated with crayons. It read, "Happy 1-Week Birthday Bella!" The kitchen table was covered with cards, frosted pink cupcakes, balloons, and, of course, pink roses. Bella quickly roused from her nap as she took in all the excitement. The children took turns holding her. They were all so gentle, tender, and loving as she was placed in their arms. Swaddled and drowsy, her yawns stirred choruses of "aah" from all, even the older boys.

All the children had visited with Bella in the NICU and had held her many times, but now they had the luxury of holding her for longer than a few minutes and without all the tubes and wires. Elizabeth, who had just celebrated her seventeenth birthday, was old enough to understand the implications of Bella's diagnosis. She appeared strained, heavyhearted, and lost in thought as she stared into the eyes of her goddaughter. Her eyes welled with tears as she told me that she was so grateful for her little angel, no matter how long she would be with us. Our fifteen-year-old, John, reacted differently. He was nervous about holding her and offered to go last. He later told me he was afraid of breaking her because she was so small.

Daniel, who was twelve, couldn't stop looking at Bella's toes and fingers; they were delicate and small as a doll's. Considering his big heart and quiet demeanor, it was little surprise that Peter tried to hold Bella the tightest. We had to remind this sweet ten-year-old that she was fragile, but he just loved her so! Our youngest boy was Patrick, age six, and he glowed with the pride of a newly crowned king. He had joined the ranks of the "big brothers" and was entirely pleased with himself. He wanted to hold her for the longest, and he talked to her about all the scary things he would protect her from: dragons, bears, and piranhas would never touch her.

Later on, our dear friend Susie came over to take a family picture of us. She was a steadfast and devoted friend who was such a great blessing to our family during this painful time. Gathering the kids, we went outside and snapped away. I remember the beauty of that spring day: the garden in bloom, the earth alive again, and the smell of honeysuckle. The heat felt welcoming as its tender touch soothed me. I had been cold for so long.

Taking a family picture is not an easy feat when you have seven kids to organize. Nonetheless, the family picture we took that day would become an important memory for us. Every physician we spoke to had said that Bella would surely die after a few days. If we were exceptionally lucky, they had said, she would live for a month. With those words ringing in my ears, I wanted a moment to capture our family while Bella was with us.

Click. Flash. Stop. The boys were in their worn T-shirts and shorts, so we had them change into something a little better and brush their hair, something I need to remind my boys to do. We went outside, where the sun was shining, and fumbled around trying to best arrange the kids. I sat in the middle of the outdoor couch, holding Bella. Sarah, Peter, and Patrick crowded next to me, eager to be as close as possible to Bella. Daniel, John, Rick, and Elizabeth stood in the back, all leaning in toward Bella.

Everyone was happy that we were having this family

picture taken but simultaneously fearful that it would some-day become a sad reminder of a fleeting period of time, a time when Bella was briefly with us. The treasured picture captured our exhaustion but also our joy, hope, and gratitude.

Even though Bella was our eighth baby, our anxiety made it seem as if she were our first. In a very real sense, we were new parents. We learned how to perform newborn care differently, more carefully, more thoughtfully. Because Bella could not nurse, I rented a pump so she could benefit from the nutritional benefits of my breast milk. We tried lots of different bottles and nipples made specifically for special-needs infants, but she got dusky every time she tried to take a bottle, because she could not suck and swallow properly. We even tried giving her oxygen when she fed, which helped, but she still wasn't able to eat enough through a bottle to sustain her. So she received her mother's milk through a nasogastric tube that went through her nose and down into her stomach. Breastfeeding was always so important to me, and it made me happy to know that Bella was healthier because of it.

Details were everything, and prayers timed all Bella's feedings. We were getting to know our Bella, her issues, and how best to take care of her. We were with Bella around the clock and watched her constantly. There were always treatments to be given and medical supplies that needed to be washed. As much as my experience as a NICU nurse helped, this was a skill set I had never dreamed I would need to use for my own baby.

Though her care was extensive, Bella was not "sickly." In fact, she acted like a normal, sleepy, newborn baby. She was a preemie, but she was growing. Other than her little fingers, only a geneticist would notice the other outward manifestations of her rare condition. We told the children that Bella was not sick; she was just made in a different but very special way. We took care of Bella as we did our other infants; we just fed her differently.

At her one-month birthday, Bella weighed five pounds, five ounces. We were proud of that simple, yet important, milestone. With her putting on weight and allowing us to measure her life in months, not weeks, we had many reasons to be hopeful. The night before this birthday, we took her to our church for the first time. In the presence of our Lord, we gave thanks for her life and resolved to continue treasuring each day with our angel.

My dear family was there for us every single day, delivering gifts, talking, praying, and helping us in every possible way. My friends Katy, Nadine, Jennifer, Leanne, Chris, Mary, Muriel, Kathy, Melanie, Laura, Katie, and, of course, Susie were all there for us. They made meals, brought Bella the sweetest baby gifts, and sat and talked. The love and support we received from our family, friends, and church community helped to strengthen and fortify us during this challenging time.

Rick wrote an e-mail on the night of Bella's one-month birthday to thank our family and friends for praying for her during her first month of life and for being there to help us. We thanked people for celebrating her life with us and for contributing to our miracle by sustaining us through prayer and support. He shared the story of how I had contacted Archbishop Chaput after hearing his homily where he mentioned our family and Bella's birth. He told me that after Mass, a woman came up to him and said she had an eleven-year-old daughter with full Trisomy 18. Her home parish was called Our Lady of Fátima—Bella's confirmation name. Rick explained that it was stories like this that had helped us keep the faith and fight the battle. Our God is a God of miracles.

We held a huge celebration for Bella's one-month birthday. Actually, it was a huge celebration in our hearts! Concerned about germs, we had a simple party with family and friends. I always say I'm so blessed to be walking through life with my family. It's a great comfort going through everything together with family, and many of our friends have shared the journey of life with us for a very long time. We have had our babies together; prayed together; celebrated baptisms, first communions, and confirmations; done sports and piano recitals together; gone on retreats together; and shared all the ups and downs of life.

God blessed us with such dear family and friends on this journey of life. Bella's one-month birthday was a joyful celebration. We had food and wine and toasted to Bella's life. We had a strawberries-and-cream cake with pink frosted roses for Bella, and almost seven years later we still have the same cake for Bella at every celebration for her. She has her own signature cake!

We built a life that summer based on new hopes and small milestones. This was the summer of simple pleasures like neighborhood walks and baseball games. Peter and Patrick were playing Little League baseball, and Rick was their coach. Their team played well that year, and I had missed watching them play, so we packed up Bella and brought her to a few games.

Bella's diaper bag was unlike any other diaper bag. It was like a physician's bag filled with gauze, syringes, tubing, and a tiny portable pulse oximetry finger probe. Standing away from the crowded bleachers, under the shade, I swayed her back and forth. Smelling clipped grass and cooking hamburgers, I smiled as I gratefully shared these peaceful moments with my little one. She was dressed in a pink dress and a sunhat as I cradled my little love tenderly. This was one of the first outfits I had bought her that wasn't a preemie size. Her wearing it was a little milestone. It sounds silly, but I was proud of her. Maybe she knew. I smiled as she cooed sweetly to herself. She loved to coo when she was drowsy, singing herself to sleep.

Peter was a catcher, and as soon as he saw me standing there with Bella, he took off his mask and grinned. Patrick spotted us from the outfield and almost ran over during the game! Rick waved him back, reminding him to keep his eye on the ball. I laughed at their sweet reactions. Peter and Patrick lost the first game Bella attended. We think they might have been a little distracted, but we had our own victories to celebrate.

Since arriving home, Bella always loved being outside. She responded to the warmth of the sun and the soft breezes. We went for walks every day, and Bella loved the birds' songs. When she heard their sweet melodies, her little legs kicked and her eyes lit up. Occasionally, she liked to sing with them, cooing and squealing her own little harmony. The walks were good for her and therapeutic for me. Frustrations and concerns were left on the side of the road.

Since being in the NICU, Psalm 23 had become my constant prayer. As I walked, I would thank God for bringing me out of the dark valley and into the light. We held Bella, sang to her, rocked her, and gave her massages. She especially loved foot massages. We would nestle her in a pillow and rub each of her feet with lavender oil while listening to the sounds of whales on her Sleep Sheep. Her feet were so tiny we only needed to massage them with one finger. Inevitably, she would relax and quickly drift off to sleep.

As she grew out of the sleepy newborn-baby phase, Bella began to interact more with us. She loved to laugh, particularly if the boys tickled her tummy or chin. She'd pull her arms to her sides, tuck in her chin, and giggle until the boys relented. Afterward, she'd inhale and exhale very deeply, like any dramatic little sister.

◆   ◆   ◆

During these first crucial months, our family, friends, and church community showered us with love, prayers, and support, active witnesses to the embracing body of Christ. They brought meals to us every day for a few months. They prayed for us, sent gifts and flowers, and helped with the children. There's something very soothing about a delicious home-cooked meal with warm, homemade bread. It was comforting to gather as a family around the table for a meal that neither Rick nor I in our exhaustion would have been able to prepare.

All these little changes helped me quickly learn that we were in a new phase of life. From the moment we brought Bella home from the NICU, one of my greatest challenges as a mom had been to make sure all my children had some "mom" time every single day. Taking care of a special-needs baby can be all-consuming, but I was the mother of seven children and needed to take care of every one of them. Night after night I would lie awake in bed, trying to process everything, and wonder how on earth I was going to do it all: sports, music lessons, playdates, plays, parent–teacher conferences for the kids who were in school, and homeschool lessons for the children at home. The list went on and on in my mind.

A dear friend of mine, Muriel, who is the mother of three special-needs children, offered some lifesaving advice. She told me to live with more simplicity, make my circle smaller, and know that "doing it all" was not possible, so I had to prioritize. From that moment on, I decided that my husband and children would literally be my entire life. A beautiful simplicity was born, and sweetness suffused everything. I had always struggled with living in the moment, and now it was just happening.

We obviously had to plan the family schedule, but now we focused on a constant awareness of the moment. Rick and I were in this together, as husband and wife, on our mission to take care of our family and nurture our marriage. We mapped out the children's activities. One of us would be with Bella, while the other was at a baseball game or school event. My friends were great at helping out with playdates and driving when Rick was busy at work.

We were on an emotional roller coaster and had to tend to our children's hearts. All my children have different ways of opening up and talking, all with their own emotional processes. I became the master of getting them to share their thoughts, which is not an easy thing to do at times! Elizabeth and Sarah liked to talk over a cup of tea; John and Daniel liked to share as we took a hike; Peter and Patrick loved snuggling on the couch and talking. One moment, one day at a time, was my motto.

As we entered into the fall and the meals from our friends stopped, cooking, something I love doing, became a huge challenge. There were many days when my kids would get home from school and ask, "Mom, what's for dinner?" and I didn't have an answer. I used to love making meals from scratch and baking bread every day, but the days were so busy that planning and meal making became next to impossible.

Through the years, our kitchen had been the heart of our home. I knew the importance of our family's gathering around the table. When we made meals, the children were always there with me, and frequently Rick would pitch in too, chopping, peeling, and stirring. My dear mother taught me how to cook; in fact, in my upbringing our kitchen was the center of our home. She was a wonderful cook and made everything from scratch. I can still hear her singing in the kitchen as we peeled garlic and chopped vegetables. I did not know any other way, and to this day I love making my mother's recipes. To put a nourishing and delicious meal on the table took a lot of time and effort. Unfortunately, this was a luxury I no longer had. Now it was shortcut time. We could not live on scrambled eggs and grilled cheese sandwiches forever.

I learned every recipe in the book. Rick's father was Italian and a great cook. He used to take many shortcuts and would say, "Why reinvent the wheel?" I took his advice. I had never used a Crock-Pot, but I broke down and bought one. I found a few slow-cooker recipe books at the Williams Sonoma outlet store. They used fresh ingredients: shallots, garlic, herbs, and wine. The delicious aromas of home-cooked meals, just like my mother made, once again infused our home.

My slow cooker saved me, because it allowed me to make dinner when there was a break in the morning or early afternoon. When the children came home from school and walked through the door, they knew Mom had something special planned for dinner. I'll never forget how wonderful it felt, when I was growing up, after a busy day at school to walk across our front lawn and into our front door to the smell of my mother's homemade bread or cookies. She made the best bread I've ever tasted, and we would have it warm out of the oven with butter. It felt so good to be doing this for my children once again.

Determined to make every minute count with Bella, we recognized the moments with her as pure gifts and worthy of joyful, grateful celebration. She continued to beat the odds. Hope grew. From the time we brought Bella home from the NICU until now, almost seven years later, Bella has been our refuge from the stress of the world. When I hold her, all life's cares and worries vanish and I'm completely caught up in the moment. She renews my perspective and gives me an optimistic outlook on life. She is a source of peace for me.

Bella is a source of peace to every person who is blessed to know her. Her peace comes from heaven and a loving Father who created her in His image. She is here for a reason, and there is no coincidence in the significance of her birth date. Bella was born on May 13, 2008, which is the feast of Our Lady of Fátima. This is an important day in the Catholic Church, because it is the day the Blessed Virgin Mary appeared to three children in Fátima, Portugal, and it's also the day Pope John Paul was shot.

On May 13, 1917, and on the thirteenth day of each of the next six months, Our Lady appeared to three shepherd children at the Cova da Iria, just outside their home village of Fátima, as they were herding sheep. The children who witnessed these apparitions were Lúcia Santos and her two cousins, Jacinta and Francisco Marto. Our Lady of Fátima asked people to do penance and to offer up sacrifices and their sufferings for peace in the world. She also asked them to pray for the conversion of sinners and for Russia to turn back to the Christian faith in order to avoid severe harm to humanity. She further stated that the First World War would end, but that a sign in the night sky would come before another world war. On January 25, 1938, a brilliant and fiery aurora borealis lit up the Northern Hemisphere and could be seen all over the world. On March 11–13, 1938, Hitler seized Austria, and then invaded Czechoslovakia eight months later.

During the last apparition, Our Lady promised a miracle to prove her messages were true. On October 13, 1917, around seventy thousand people gathered and witnessed the Miracle of the Sun, when the sun "danced" in the sky. Even anticlerical, non-Christian reporters described the sun as full of brilliant colors and trembling, whirling, and dancing in the sky, defying "cosmic laws."[1]

On the sixty-fourth anniversary of the apparitions, May 13, 1981, a Turkish gunman shot Pope John Paul II. The pope had a deep devotion to the Virgin Mary and was looking at a picture of her when the militant shot him. Earlier in the day, the pope had met with Dr. Jerome Lejeune, the geneticist who discovered Trisomy 21. Dr. Lejeune was a great advocate for people with Trisomy 21. It was also on that same day that Pope John Paul II started the institute for the study of marriage and the family, and the Communist Party's pro-abortion march was canceled.

After being shot, Pope John Paul suffered immensely. He experienced serious pain and other medical issues because of the injury. Through it all, he taught the world about suffering.

He taught us that suffering brings us closer to Christ. John 16:33 says, "In the world you will have tribulation. But take heart; I have overcome the world."

I don't claim to understand the significance of Bella's birth date, but I do know that God does; He chose it. Bella's full name is Isabella Maria. *Isabella* means "consecrated to God," and *Maria* refers to the Blessed Virgin Mary, who teaches us the joy of saying yes to God's invitation of love. Mary, the mother of the Lord Jesus Christ.

Mary's yes, in what would certainly have been called a crisis pregnancy in our day, speaks loudly to an age in which the beauty of every life is all but forgotten. And like Mary, our little girl is filled with grace. She is a gift—a treasure from heaven—and her life is teaching us the meaning of love's invitation. Bella's life has affirmed the messages of Fátima, and through prayer and sacrifice we have drawn closer to Christ and felt His bountiful love.

6

LOVE IS
PERSISTENT

◆ Karen Santorum ◆

Death and life are in the power of the tongue.

—PROVERBS 18:21

I n the summer of 2008, our family began a new journey together as we learned how to love and care for Bella. The doctors had sent Bella home from the NICU on hospice. Care for the dying for our newborn baby—a painful paradox. The hospice nurse who visited Bella once a week was kind and understanding, yet there was a somber darkness surrounding her coming, simply for the reason that hospice doesn't invest in life; it prepares for death. Though she was kind, I dreaded her visits. She brought pamphlets about coffins, funerals, and grave sites. "It's always best to be prepared," she'd say as she showed me the different types of marble for a tombstone. *Tombstone.* The word bludgeoned my heart.

Hospice offered no pediatric supplies. The few items we did receive for Bella's everyday care were the wrong size—made for adults and not for a preemie baby. I remember opening a box, thankful for a new shipment of nasogastric tubes, just as Bella was running out. Upon opening the first bag, I realized the tubes were for an adult and far too thick and long to insert into my baby's tiny nose. My hands began to shake. We were fighting for life; they had settled for death. So many obstacles. Even obtaining those life-giving supplies became another battle.

Rick heard me as I cried out in desperation, and he came in, wearing a confused look of concern. He saw me staring at the box, lip trembling as I cried out: "These are all adult sizes!" Rick simply hugged me as I cried. I immediately called our pediatrician, Dr. James Baugh, and described our situation. Fortunately, his office gave us a few NG tubes from their medical supplies closet. I felt alone, as though crawling up a shale-covered mountain. No summit in sight. No healing.

Other obstacles to hope were the "professional articles" filled with statistical predictions of how long Trisomy 18 children live but offering no advice about how to help them stay alive. Much of my time was spent on the phone, fighting for supplies, talking with doctors, and trying to remain calm while battling my way through all the answering machines at the insurance company and our physicians' offices. Eventually

I got smart and started ordering medical supplies and necessities, and Bella's clothes, online. She was tiny and needed preemie clothes. I ordered her some adorable preemie clothes when she came home from the NICU.

Bella was our little love, and we wanted her to have soft sleepers with whimsical princesses, bears, and bunnies. After placing the order, I sat at my computer and cried, wondering if the clothes would get here in time for Bella to wear them. Anytime someone gave us an outfit for six months or nine months, I would sigh and hurt inside, thinking she might never grow big enough or live long enough to wear the outfit.

I brought the sadness from the NICU home with me, but it was time to be positive and count the blessings. The doctors explained to us how best to prepare for Bella's death; instead, we chose to celebrate her life. And we did, every single day. From the "Happy Birthday Bella" sign to the pink roses (Bella's favorite), balloons, and cupcakes. We had a "birthday" party every week.

My daughter Elizabeth, who is wise beyond her years, said to me shortly after our return home, "Mom, Bella knows when you're sad and crying. We should be happy while she's with us." She was absolutely right. Even the smallest infants, and all our children, feel a parent's emotions and are affected by them. Her words struck me, and my attitude changed. From that moment on, we decided to focus on Bella's life. We lived in celebration of the blessings that came from her life. We would not preemptively mourn her predicted death.

We began doing *well* baby visits. It was a refreshing change to focus completely on Bella's health and helping her through her medical issues, rather than talk about grave sites. I ordered two books from the SOFT (Support Organization for

Trisomy 18, 13, and Related Disorders) website about caring for a baby with Trisomy 18. They offered valuable advice that we used to guide us in Bella's daily care and her doctor visits. I ordered extra copies for our pediatrician, Dr. James Baugh, which he appreciated, since he had never cared for an infant with Trisomy 18. He made house calls and took great care of Bella. As always, he was kind, thoughtful, and compassionate. Bella was gaining weight and on the growth chart for normal babies. She wasn't just surviving; she was thriving!

During one of Dr. Baugh's visits to our home, I asked him to double-check a dose of morphine that the hospice doctor had prescribed. The day after Bella's arrival home, the hospice doctor and nurse had visited and explained in cold, graphic detail that Bella would need this morphine when she "began to fail." The hospice physician had told us with certainty that Bella would go into either cardiac or respiratory arrest and would be cyanotic and restless, gasping for breath, and eventually, her breathing and her heart would stop. Rick and I had made sure the children were outside so they would not hear any of this conversation. They were running around in the yard playing freeze tag and laughing. Rick and I were wondering how we were going to hold it together when they came inside.

Holding on to our tiny love, we sat there in our family room, bleary-eyed, exhausted, and barely able to listen to something so horrible. As I listened to the chilling scene the hospice doctor described, I desperately cried out to our Lord for help and comfort, repeating *help me, Jesus* over and over in my mind. That was the prayer, so simple, but so very important.

C. S. Lewis said, "What may seem our worst prayers may

really be, in God's eyes, our best. Those, I mean, which are least supported by devotional feeling. For these may come from a deeper level than feeling. God sometimes seems to speak to us most intimately when he catches us, as it were, off our guard."

As a NICU nurse, I understood the therapeutic effect of morphine in a cardiac or respiratory arrest situation, but I also knew too high a dose would be lethal. Dr. Baugh took the bottle of morphine and turned pale. He could barely get the words out of his mouth as he shook his head, "Well, that *is* a high dose." He explained that it would have been a lethal dose. That moment confirmed we were navigating our way through a battlefield where there were enemies and allies. I canceled hospice immediately and felt a huge sense of relief and joy.

◆   ◆   ◆

After Bella's birth, my dear mom, dad, and sister, Maureen, came to visit us twice. Rick's parents came to visit us too. Our parents were in their eighties at the time. My dad was in the early phase of Alzheimer's disease and Rick's father was in a wheelchair, so traveling was difficult, but the fact they made the long trips meant the world to my family. Our parents' and sister's love and support were like an oasis in the desert. They acknowledged Bella as a person—as a member of our family. They held her ever so gently, talked to her in sweet whispers, and loved her with all their hearts. Many pictures captured those moments. Their hugs comforted all the children.

My dad was a distinguished physician and geneticist, but when we needed his advice and guidance with Trisomy 18, he had lost much of his memory to Alzheimer's disease. Yet, one night, as we sat on the back porch, my dad recalled a little girl at our church who had Trisomy 18 and had lived to be six years old. My mom nodded in agreement. She remembered her too. This small memory lifted our spirits and gave us one more simple reason to hope. My brother, Jim, and his wife, Anna, told us about a girl they knew in Spain who has Trisomy 18. She is older, and they said she is happy and doing really well. This meant the world to Rick and me.

●　　◆　　●

Since Bella's birth, we had been fervently praying for a miracle, and we believe she received one at her one-month visit with the cardiologist. Bella had two large VSDs (ventricular septal defects), holes in her heart, that were diagnosed in the NICU. Waiting for the results of this one-month echocardiogram, our hearts were heavy, fearful we were going to be told Bella would need surgery or that she would develop pulmonary hypertension or cyanosis. Instead, the cardiologist, Dr. Mary Donofrio, entered the exam room with a huge smile on her face and told Rick and me the holes in Bella's heart had closed! Praise God! Before we left, she said with confidence, "I'll see you in a year for Bella's follow-up." For the first time since her birth, we burst into tears of joy. No one had ever given Bella a future like that.

The transition from the NICU to trying to establish a new normal way of life was a strange time. Activities that had never been a big deal suddenly became a huge challenge, like simply going to the grocery store and running errands. For the first couple of months after Bella came home from the NICU, I did not go anywhere except to church. I was completely consumed with taking care of Bella, my six other children, and my dear husband. There were days when just taking a shower or brushing my hair seemed almost impossible.

Bella needed to be fed every two hours, and it seemed as though I would finish one round of care only to go right into the next. Bella had to be fed slowly with a syringe through her NG tube, and so I timed each milliliter of milk with a prayer. In between Bella's feedings we gave her baby massages, bathed and dressed her, washed her medical supplies, and I pumped breast milk. Bella was always in someone's arms, and we knew she felt the love. Fortunately, by the time Bella came home from the hospital, our kids had finished school and were able to help out with chores and driving.

I was completely exhausted, and it was a huge challenge keeping the kids' lives as normal as possible with their usual routines: music lessons, sports, and friends. As time passed, we realized we were living in a completely different world, and things that used to matter no longer did. C. S. Lewis, in *A Grief Observed*, said, "Perhaps the bereaved ought to be isolated in special settlements like lepers." So funny and so true!

There was no real normal anymore, and I was trying to figure out what our new life looked like and how we would live. It was as if my happy, organized life had been swept up in a tornado and then thrown all over the ground, and we had to pick up the pieces and make sense of everything. Little by little, we figured life out one day at a time. My emotions were like a pendulum, swinging from joy and gratitude that Bella was doing well, to grief and despair over the concern for her health and medical issues.

There was also a sadness in my heart that we could not go to Mass as a family. We loved being at Mass together, praying as a family and then talking with our friends after Mass. When I went to church, I sat in the back, clinging to my phone, afraid of getting a call about Bella being in a crisis, and I cried the entire time. After Mass, I exited quickly to get back to Bella.

One day after Mass, there was an ambulance rushing by my car and heading in the same direction as my home. This triggered a flood of tears and emotion; I was convinced it was going to my home. When I returned, my dear Rick, as always, held me and calmed my anxious heart.

When we brought Bella home from the NICU, a dear friend of ours, who has a special-needs child, told us that this time would be hard on our marriage if we did not hold tight *together*. She said to never forget that "you are husband and wife—you are lovers." Rick and I promised each other the gift of time to nurture our marriage every day. Whether it was a walk through the neighborhood, a drink on the porch, or reading together around the fire, we actively planned time to talk with, listen to, and love each other.

And so, when our special girl entered into our lives, we continued to do what we had always done; no matter what the day might bring, Rick and I make time for each other and take care of each other. "I will seek him whom my soul loves" (Song 3:2). This promise has made all the difference in our marriage. Bella has made our marriage even stronger. All the ups and downs of life have made us closer and have deepened our unity and love for each other.

◆   ◆   ◆

When Bella was two and a half months old, her pediatrician told us she would need a feeding button. Bella was taking some breast milk by mouth, but not enough to sustain her. Most of her nutrition came through the nasogastric tube, but as Bella got older, she began to pull on it. We were concerned about her aspirating if she suddenly pulled out the tube during a feeding. We met with two local physicians who performed this type of surgery, and they both said our baby would never survive the surgery. At both appointments, I reminded the doctor that my baby's name is Bella, but that did not seem to matter, and they did not refer to her by name. Their reactions told me that because of Bella's diagnosis, they weren't even considering the surgery.

To them Bella was a liability, at best, and, at worst, she simply wasn't worth the effort. These appointments were definitely momma bear moments. I knew that I would never think, even for a moment, of putting my dear baby into their care. If the physician believed Bella would not survive the surgery, then the outcome could likely be just that. I wanted a physician who was positive and believed in Bella and hoped for her.

When Jesus was here on earth, He healed the sick. He did not disregard them or throw them away or say, "You will have a poor quality of life, so I will not care for you." Rather, Jesus said, "Go and tell John what you hear and see: the blind receive their sight and the lame walk, lepers are cleansed and the deaf hear, and the dead are raised up, and the poor have good news preached to them" (Matt. 11:4–5). The apostle Mark wrote of Him, "He has done all things well; he even makes the deaf hear and the dumb speak" (Mark 7:37). It was the weak, the fragile members of society, whom Jesus made the focus of His care and attention. "So the last will be first, and the first last" (Matt. 20:16).

The Gospel of John describes Jesus healing a blind man: "As he passed by, he saw a man blind from his birth. And his disciples asked him, 'Rabbi, who sinned, this man or his parents, that he was born blind?' Jesus answered, 'It was not that this man sinned or his parents, but that the works of God might be made manifest in him' " (John 9:1–3). During that time in Israel, people assumed that such afflictions were brought on by sin or uncleanness. Jesus made it clear that no one was responsible for the man's blindness; rather, he was blind so that God's providence could be shown through him. Like the blind man, Bella is here so that "the works of God can be made manifest in [her]." God has a plan for Bella's life. There is a reason why Bella, and all of us, are made in such unique ways. God has a purpose for all of us.

The verdict from the icy people who called themselves physicians left me with a heavy heart, and I stayed up all night crying as feelings of devastation overwhelmed me. Even the smallest challenges of Bella's care sent me into dead-end alleyways. I had to and I wanted to scale walls to care for her. And I was exhausted. My heart was weary, pushed to the breaking point.

In those moments when the soul is stripped of hope, the frantic desperation one feels is akin to Job-like madness. Venturing into uncharted, stormy seas, my vessel was my faith, and it separated me from the sea of madness and sorrow. In different moments, I resented the vessel for not being strong enough to calm the storms.

The day after our appointment with the last doctor we had visited, Rick helped me pick up the pieces. Together we were resolved and strong. We would find a team of physicians to care for Bella. After all, we would never put our child into the hands of physicians who didn't see her as a valuable, beautiful life. Rick and I called Dr. Scott Adzick, a friend of ours at the Children's Hospital of Philadelphia (CHOP) and one of the most impressive surgeons in the world. He is kind and compassionate. He recommended Dr. Thane Blinman, a brilliant surgeon who has spent years perfecting many surgeries laproscopically.

Dr. Blinman could not have been nicer, and he referred to Bella by name. This sounds like such a small detail, but in the world of people with disabilities, a name gives hope. He acknowledged her life, her person, and gave her value by saying her name.

Dr. Blinman wanted to know about Bella and her needs, something the other doctors had never even asked. At the end of a long and compassionate conversation, Dr. Blinman said he had several Trisomy 18 patients and believed Bella would do really well. And she did. Bella had the surgery at CHOP when she was three months old, and there was no problem getting her on or off the ventilator, no infection, and no problem with her feedings. Dr. Blinman did the surgery laparoscopically, and in one procedure Bella had the feeding button in place. She was home in two days. Bella is almost seven years old now, and she's never had an issue with her feeding button.

Until Bella was five, we went up to CHOP every three months and then every six months since. Bella sees all her physicians and her nutritionist, Robin Cook, whose cheerful demeanor always made our visits with her so pleasant. She would quickly calculate Bella's nutritional needs, giving us guidance with every detail of Bella's feedings, such as vitamins, minerals, fiber, calories, and fluids. Dr. Blinman and Robin work together with us on Bella's nutritional needs. Dr. Blinman's disarming sense of humor and Robin's vivacity still light up the hospital room. Both Robin and Dr. Blinman have played pivotal roles in our journey with Bella, and we are so grateful to know them.

At CHOP, the doctors approached Bella optimistically, with compassion and respect. While other doctors said Bella would never talk or walk, physicians at CHOP said, "Bella communicates well with her eyes and facial expressions. She has good muscle tone and, with the proper therapy, may be able to use a walker." While local doctors told us Bella's face was abnormally small and would give her breathing problems, doctors at CHOP said Bella was beautiful and her sweet face was petite. They told us they could help her breathe better.

While other doctors commented that her mouth was too small, a doctor in CHOP's PICU told us that she loved Bella's little mouth and would find an oxygen mask that fit just perfectly. Not only did they see her beauty, but they also recognized her potential and wanted to help her reach it. While other doctors were saying there was no hope, CHOP physicians were saying to just give her a chance.

Almost seven years have passed since Bella's birth. Nearly seven years since we received the crushing diagnosis of Trisomy 18. Virtually seven years since those words "lethal diagnosis" and "incompatible with life" were coldly spoken by the doctor and burned into our hearts. Was it a slip of the tongue? Maybe the doctor just didn't think before he spoke. Maybe he just didn't realize the huge impact his words would have. After almost seven years, they still disturb me and echo in my mind as if they had just been spoken.

As the mother of seven children, I know how powerful

words can be, and I tend to obsess over which words I use in various situations with my children. "Pleasant words are like a honeycomb, sweetness to the soul and health to the body" (Prov. 16:24). Words can affirm, encourage, and inspire, or they can frustrate, degrade, and build anger. Through the years I have known what it means to my children when I encourage and validate them with positive words. I have read parenting books about how our words will have lasting effects on our children, and I regret the times I have carelessly spoken without thinking. I know all of us have said things we wish we hadn't.

These doctors, however, seemed to have no remorse over the toxic words they used. Maybe they had taken the line right out of a medical book or their medical school professors had used these words.

When Bella was three and a half, she was hospitalized for pneumonia. A few days into her stay, she was sitting up in her bed, playing with her toys. A young physician who had been assisting in her care stood at the foot of her bed. He was watching Bella, and she looked up at him. She kept smiling and giggling. I looked over at this tall, athletic physician and was surprised to see tears running down his face. When I asked if he was all right, he said, "I didn't know kids like Bella existed. All we were told in medical school was kids with Trisomy 18 never lived. I feel so lied to."

I wish that doctors, like parents, would choose their words more carefully and understand that when they say "lethal diagnosis" it can too often lead to deadly outcomes. "Death and life are in the power of the tongue" (Prov. 18:21). God Himself instructs us to use caution with the words we choose to use.

Rick and I are not alone in this experience. During the

past seven years, I have become immersed in the world of Trisomy parents and their children. I frequently talk or correspond with parents. I have read every article and watched every video I could find. What I have learned is that doctors always refer to Trisomy 18 infants as having a "lethal diagnosis" and always say that the children are "incompatible with life." All the Trisomy 18 parents I have spoken with have faced this same battle. The only place where we did not hear Trisomy 18 referred to as "lethal" or "incompatible with life" was at the Children's Hospital of Philadelphia.

When parents hear the word *lethal*, it places fear into their minds and gives them a sense of hopelessness. When we watch the nightly news, we hear about people dying from lethal attacks, lethal weapons, and lethal drug doses. In all those situations, the people are already dead, and we are learning about what lethal thing killed them. To refer to a child who is still alive as having a "lethal diagnosis" is grossly inaccurate; many children who have Trisomy 18 survive and thrive, even into adulthood.

> *The tongue of the wise dispenses knowledge,*
> *but the mouths of fools pour out folly.*
> *A gentle tongue is a tree of life.*
> (PROV. 15:2, 4)

Moreover, any good physician knows that a thorough patient exam and evaluation is necessary to make an accurate diagnosis. After reviewing the patient's history and analyzing the tests and labs, then a physician can come to a conclusion. Making a diagnosis should be a thoughtful process. Sadly and too often in the Trisomy world, a physician will get the

Trisomy 18 results from an amniocentesis or blood tests and quickly write the child off without any further evaluation as to what his or her issues are. It's a sweeping assumption that is careless and irresponsible.

Trisomy 18 is a serious diagnosis, but physicians need to first look at their patients and see what the issues are before disregarding the infant and eliminating all hope. If they fail to do this, they abandon their patients and should not be practicing physicians. Patients deserve better. A friend of mine once said that "the MD after their name does not stand for 'Medical Deity'!" I wish doctors would realize they should not be playing God.

What follows after a Trisomy 18 diagnosis is the long, drawn-out, bleak list of what the child will surely suffer from and will not ever be able to do. It's the "will never" list. Rick and I painfully sat through the "will never" list many times, hearts heavy, but hopeful that Bella would prove them all wrong. We were told Bella would never sit up, never walk, never know us, never talk, and that she would be a vegetable who would never live past a month at most. But, essentially seven years later, Bella does know us. She plays with her toys and frequently looks up and smiles. She is a spunky girl who loves being silly and making everyone around her laugh. She has her favorite music that she loves listening and dancing to, and she loves books.

Bella walks all the way across the kitchen floor in her walker. She works hard at walking and knows she's done something great when we tell her how proud we are of her. She may not speak English, but she speaks "Bellish" quite well, and we always know what she's saying. Like any of our children, Bella is her own unique person and will do things in her own way, in her own time. We think she's perfect and love her just the way she is! But the fact is that what Bella (or any other person with special needs) "can do" does not determine her value. What truly matters is that Bella and other children like her are all created in the image of God. My prayer is that they be treated with love, dignity, and respect, not dismissed and left to die.

◆   ◆   ◆

The summer of 2008 was the summer of small miracles: firing hospice, Bella's g-button surgery, and figuring out how to balance family life. These small miracles were wondrous affirmations of God's compassionate hand acting in our broken world. C. S. Lewis wrote, "Miracles are a retelling in small letters of the very same story which is written across the whole world in letters too large for some of us to see."

As the summer months went by, the "Happy Birthday Bella" sign still hung in the doorway. Determined to make every minute count with Bella, we recognized those moments as pure gifts and worthy of joyful, grateful celebration. As the weeks went by, we changed the birthday sign from one to two to three weeks. Eventually weeks turned into months and months turned into years. Bella continued to beat the odds. Hope endured. Bella's story is small and simple, but perhaps that purity makes it possible for us to see the miracle of her life. Her large life is written in small letters.

7

LOVE IS HEROIC

• *Rick Santorum* •

Heroism is endurance for one moment more.

—GEORGE F. KENNAN

When I hear the word *heroic*, my mind conjures up images of a soldier single-handedly taking out an enemy position or those New York City firefighters rushing into the World Trade Center on September 11.

Webster's Dictionary defines *heroic* as, among other things, "brave, courageous, extremely noble and self-sacrificing."

To some degree, all parents engage in acts of heroism in raising their children, because we disregard our own desires to meet their needs. The superhero in our house under that definition is Karen, the love of my life and my wife.

When I met Karen, she was a second-year law student who was working part-time as a nurse. She graduated from law school a week before our wedding with a job in hand to clerk for a federal judge in Pittsburgh. She delayed the start of the clerkship to knock on doors with me in what every political observer, and I mean every one of them, believed was a quixotic run for US Congress.

After our miraculous win, Karen was all set to start her legal career. Unfortunately, just after the election the federal judge rescinded his offer to Karen. It turned out the judge, who was a Democratic activist before being appointed by the court, was a good friend of the congressman we defeated. Since he approved her delayed start until after the election, we assumed he was going to honor his offer. It turned out the offer was good only if I did what he expected of me—lose.

You might be thinking, *no big deal.* She was a law review graduate of a well-respected law school in town, the University of Pittsburgh, plus the wife of a congressman. Piece of cake! That may have been true if it weren't for her physical condition. We had found out just before Labor Day that Karen was expecting our first child, Elizabeth.

Karen wanted to continue working until the baby came. Back then, Pittsburgh was a tough town for women in the workplace, much less pregnant ones, even tougher on Republicans, and toughest yet on the wife of that conservative upstart, Rick Santorum.

We decided that after a grueling election, my starting a new job that would take me out of town three days most weeks and getting ready for our first child in that environment would max out the stress meter.

And so it was, from the very beginning of our marriage, Karen put her professional dreams on hold to put family first and help me pursue my calling. That was only the beginning. She was an integral part of two campaigns for Congress, three campaigns for the United States Senate, and a national election for president, during which we personally campaigned in twenty-five states before exiting the race.

She not only held down the fort, but in several of the campaigns—particularly our first race for the House and even more so during our first Senate race—she hit the campaign trail. In 1994 the biggest issue in our campaign was health care because my general election opponent was the Senate sponsor of "Hillarycare." Karen was a neonatal intensive care nurse with a law degree, with an emphasis on health law. She turned out to be our secret weapon, traveling the state and giving her strong and well-grounded arguments against government-run health care.

Then there was the daily heroism of being a mother at home. There is no more important and fulfilling, while at the same time humbling and at times demeaning, job than running a household. Karen dedicated herself to it every day, and thanks to my campaigns and serving in the House and Senate, they were long days.

During our first four years in the House, we kept our home outside of Pittsburgh. We rented an apartment in Alexandria, and Karen and I would drive back and forth to DC every week for session. After I was reelected in 1992, our son John was born, and it became a bit more of an ordeal to travel back and forth. We also decided right after that election to take a leap of faith and run for the United States Senate in Pennsylvania.

Because of the proximity of Philadelphia and Harrisburg to DC, I knew there would be many a night that I would travel up to the state to campaign. We decided to keep the family at home in Mt. Lebanon and I would sleep at "Club Fed," as we called it. Many members of Congress who, like us, did not come to Washington with a hefty balance sheet, slept in their offices and used the House gym locker room to shower and get ready for the next day. What that meant for Karen, of course, was more time on her own caring for two children.

We finally moved to Northern Virginia after a year in the Senate, trying to go back and forth to our home in Pittsburgh and living in an apartment in Arlington. It seemed as if we were on the road between Pittsburgh and DC half of our life; and first with two, then with three children under age four, it was too much. We had to decide where to plant the family for my time in the Senate.

It was not an easy decision. While my family had all moved away from Western Pennsylvania, Karen still had living there her parents, nine of ten siblings, and some thirty nieces and nephews. They are a tight-knit family who get together all the time and are very supportive of each other. Again Karen put our marriage and family first in 1995, and we moved into a home in Herndon, Virginia, about twenty miles outside of DC.

The 2012 presidential race was a difficult and stressful journey, but for sheer effort and time away from family, the 1994 Senate race was the worst. I'll never forget an incident that was a wake-up call during that year of transition in my life, 1995. Karen and I were changing out clothes for the kids, and Karen pulled out a pair of boy's pajamas and said, "Aah . . . Johnny loved these pajamas; he wore them to bed almost every night."

I looked at the pajamas and said, "I don't recall ever seeing those!" I vowed then never to let anything consume me as that race had done. That moment helped send me on a different path to be a better husband, father, and follower of Jesus Christ.

In Virginia, our lives slowed down some, but the days were still long, and there was the constant travel to Pennsylvania. I pledged to visit every county every year, and I did so for my twelve years in office. Karen was always there, supporting this time-consuming job.

Our children were now getting to be of school age, and we had to make a decision on schools. We were still traveling back and forth to Pittsburgh on a regular basis on weekends, and during the weeks the Senate was not in session. If we put Elizabeth in school, that travel would be dramatically curtailed. In addition, when I was in DC, I was routinely gone from the house at 5:30 a.m. and didn't get home until 8:00 p.m. Karen began looking into the possibility of teaching the kids at home. After much prayer and research, we decided to give it a shot for just one year.

It worked out beautifully for everyone that year, so we decided to try one more year, adding John to the mix. We ended up making eighteen one-year commitments to school at home, and it has made all the difference for our family. We have an incredible bond with our children that I would have never had given my schedule. Teaching the children at home allowed our family life to be in rhythm with my Senate schedule. With the exception of one year when I solo taught Daniel in first grade, Karen carried the vast majority of the responsibility for educating our children.

After Gabriel's death in 1996, we had three more children. In spite of the craziness that comes with caring for a hockey team–sized clan, Karen and I were hoping for even more. We realized that as much as you love the first child, and you don't think you could possibly love another child as much, you do. Each child, I think, increases your capacity to love, so we hoped for God to continue to bless us with more children. Eventually, with time the window of opportunity for another baby closed, and we accepted the fact that God had no more children for us. That's when God surprised us with a very special gift.

• • •

When Bella arrived and we learned the news of her condition, Karen went into a gear I had only glimpsed over the years. "Momma Bear" doesn't begin to describe how she cared for her miracle baby. She was determined to give Bella the perfect environment in which to thrive, starting with a germ-free home. I wish I had been wise enough in May 2008 to buy stock in Johnson & Johnson, the makers of Purell hand sanitizer, because we bought it by the case! Karen made sure we all washed our hands before holding Bella, and if there was no water around, we used hand sanitizer.

Karen and I both spent hours on the Internet trying to gather information, but we found the best source was talking with other T18 families. Bob and Heather Mylod were particularly helpful. I saw Bob's father at a small meeting of Catholics in Baltimore when Bella was just a few weeks old, and I shared the news with him. He told me about the blessing of his two-and-a-half-year-old granddaughter, Vivi, and how she was so full of life. After reading all the tragic stories on T18 websites, we needed some hope!

And hope is what they delivered. Their first advice was to not read anything about T18 online! Second, they said we should find a team of doctors who would fight for Bella as they would for any other child. While it is true that many T18 children do not survive long, their deaths are, in many cases, a self-fulfilling prophecy. We discovered the medical community often writes off these children. Parents are advised to do nothing or to simply provide comfort care, which ultimately denies these children lifesaving treatments.

Heather and Bob gave us hope that maybe, just maybe, if we provided Bella with the best possible care and surrounded her with constant love and prayed for a miracle, she, too, could live to the age of two and a half or older. They also provided insights on every aspect of their care for Vivi, but the most important thing that struck me as I listened to them was that they were completely devoted to their daughter. You could just feel the love coming through the phone.

Vivi was another precious member of their family who, like every child, brings joy and hardship. I must admit I didn't see that right away. I was still too focused on managing the rest of my family's anxiety.

Another angel who blessed our family was the mother of Peter Kellett. Her name is Mary, and Karen heard about her organization, Prenatal Partners for Life, from a mutual friend. Like the Mylods, Mary and her family are strong believers whose faith was challenged but ultimately enriched by carrying the cross of a T18 child. Peter was almost two, but Mary was full of what seemed like a lifetime of information to help us gain confidence in caring for Bella.

When Bella was four years old, I was the featured speaker at a fund-raising event for Prenatal Partners for Life and had the chance to meet Bella's T18 friend Peter and many of Mary's other children. I sat with Peter on my lap, just as I hold my Bella, and so many of his mannerisms caught me by surprise. I had thought they were unique to Bella, but Peter moved and sounded just like her. He was so cute.

I met many more moms and a few dads at the banquet afterward and heard story after story of their heroic efforts to care for these fragile children. Almost all the stories involved battles with doctors and hospitals to get more than the merely palliative care called for in the medical literature. But of all the stories, one sticks with me to this day.

This was a woman—let's call her Rene—from Canada, who told of her experience with her daughter, Annie, with T18. The beginning sounded just like Bella—in the NICU, doing well. As with Bella, the doctors told the family there were no life-threatening issues. Annie's tests were normal, and they sent her home because there was nothing more they could do for her at the hospital.

For the first few weeks, everything seemed normal, but Rene began noticing a gradual decline in Annie's health because of respiratory difficulty. She went to the doctor, but the doctor urged her to take a conservative approach to see if Annie would improve without treatment. After about three months, Annie's condition declined rapidly. I saw a picture of Annie taken a week before she died. Her face was red and puffy as if she had been holding her breath for two minutes.

When Rene went back to the doctor, he said it was probably just a reaction to medication.

As I was listening to this story, all I kept thinking was that this was what we might have to deal with someday. Rene was describing what the doctors said would likely kill Bella, some sort of respiratory failure or disease. My heart was breaking for her, but Rene was also cranking up my anxiety for our little Bella.

As Annie's condition worsened, Rene brought her to the hospital. There she was diagnosed with severe hypercapnia, a buildup of carbon dioxide in her blood. Hypercapnia can be treated, but her levels were so severe that she died within hours.

Rene, as you could imagine, had struggled with losing Annie. Annie had seemed to be doing so well, other than the lung issues. Rene had to get some answers beyond the typical "T18 children just don't live long." That she knew. What Rene had to find out was why Annie died.

The first clue to this tale came from the coroner's report. It stated that Annie had a "do not resuscitate order" when she was admitted to the hospital, even though no one in the family had consented to such an order.

Remember, Rene lives in Canada, which has a single-payer, government-run health system—think the Department of Motor Vehicles, only this time it's lifesaving treatment, not your license you are waiting for. After a protracted dispute in which the hospital refused to release Annie's records to her parents, Annie's records were released. The records revealed a tragic story of deliberate neglect by a team of medical professionals who were charged with her care. The first set of tests on her before she was released from the hospital after her birth showed that she was retaining CO_2!

It turned out that the only people who didn't know Annie was dying of CO_2 poisoning were her family. It seems the medical team had determined her life was not worth the expenditure of scarce government resources. And since T18 children don't generally live long, they felt that letting her slowly suffocate while her parents were kept in the dark about her condition was a humane way to euthanize her.

Annie's story could never happen in America, you say. We are on our way to such a state, however, with a lethal combination of increased government control and a progressively utilitarian view of life. As America transitions from a private health care system to one of government command and control under the Affordable Care Act, we need to keep in mind that in a private system the patient is a profit center; in a government-run system the patient is a cost center. In which system would you want to be a patient—one that is incentivized to provide care or one that is predisposed to delay and deny medical care?

This story was actually one of the reasons Karen and I decided to throw my hat in the ring for president in 2012. As the father of a child with both mental and physical impairments, I knew Bella and her peers would be the first to have their care ratcheted back. I felt that winning the White House and stopping the implementation of the Affordable Care Act was the best way to save Bella and so many other children like her from this horrible fate.

Believe it or not, these anecdotes from parents of T18 children were the best aid in coping with all that comes with

T18. But as much as you can prepare, there is nothing like experience as a teacher.

◆   ◆   ◆

From May to September of the first year of her life, Bella was cruising, but a simple sniffle turned our lives upside down. Parents and doctors told us repeatedly that a cold would be a life-threatening event for Bella. As much as I thought I understood their worries, we were totally unprepared when it happened.

When autumn came, Karen battened down the hatches to keep Bella away from any germs. Even though she had had a great summer and had gained a good amount of weight for a baby with her condition, she was still barely on the growth charts. In spite of the precautions, she woke up one morning with a runny nose. That night was a tough night, as the cold started to go to her chest. While we were incredibly worried, she seemed to be handling it like our other babies.

When we awoke the next morning, she had stopped crying and whining, but her breathing became labored. Karen quickly called her sister Kathy, who is a pediatrician, to seek counsel. Karen checked Bella's heart rate, and it was down to sixty, which for a little baby is low, but for a sick baby is very low. I was sitting next to Karen as she held Bella and talked with her sister, and it was clear our baby girl was struggling to breathe.

Karen gave Bella oxygen with a face mask. Then I remember Karen saying that Bella was getting dusky even though she had increased the oxygen. I noticed she was working hard to breathe but was not sure she was actually getting any air in her lungs. At this early point in Bella's life, she did not yet have a heart rate and pulse oximetry monitor. Karen listened with her stethoscope again, and this time Bella's heart rate was thirty. She had stopped breathing. Karen immediately started CPR to revive Bella, and I grabbed the phone and called 911.

Karen is an awesome nurse. She had worked in one of the busiest neonatal intensive care units in the country for nine years and never lost a patient on her shift. She not only has great skills, but she also has such a loving heart of compassion for children. I know every one of those children she cared for felt her love. It's one thing to put your skills to work on the job; it is another to gather your wits and be able to administer CPR properly to a tiny baby who is your own daughter. As I was on the phone, talking to the dispatcher, giving him all the information I could, I was marveling at how Karen, panic-stricken and a ball of nerves, was holding it together to help Bella breathe until the EMTs arrived.

Thankfully, we were fewer than five minutes from the local ambulance station, and they arrived in minutes. They hooked Bella up to a monitor. Her pulse had returned to normal, but she had less-than-optimal oxygen levels. Praise God, she was still with us. By the time Karen and the team hopped in the ambulance to take her to the hospital, she had stabilized.

When it comes to Bella, Karen and I are in sync—hospitals may give great care, but we only go there as an absolutely last resort. Nothing against hospitals, but there are just too many sick people around with all sorts of bugs worse than what you came in with. So, four days later Bella came home from the hospital, and while she was not back to good as new, she was home. She was still on oxygen to help her breathe because her lungs were not fully recovered, but she was our smiling, happy girl again. We felt as if we had dodged a bullet. So many of the children we had heard about from our friends had horror stories of long stays, ventilators, and even surgeries.

We brought a few new medical devices from the hospital to help us take care of Bella at home. Since she was still on oxygen, we needed a pulse oximeter to monitor her heart rate and the oxygen levels in her blood. At first I hated that machine; I was so worried about Bella that I just couldn't take my eyes off it. When it alarmed—day or night, awake or asleep—we would make a beeline to check that she was okay. Ninety-nine percent of the time she would be fine, but with Bella we knew that it only takes once. Later we realized what a godsend that machine was.

She was fine for a few weeks, but it was taking a long time to wean her off the oxygen, particularly at night. Then one afternoon in early November, the sniffles started and by nightfall she was having trouble breathing through her nose, though her chest was clear. We started her on medication and prayed it would take hold before she got too sick.

We prayed that the cold would not go into her chest, but by morning the coughing and wheezing had started. We knew what that meant. We had to watch her blood oxygen levels, and if she couldn't keep them above ninety-four on the pulse oximeter, we would have to take her in. I can't stress enough how much we wanted to avoid going to the hospital. It wasn't just the infections; it was also a concern about the care she would receive. We had heard so many horror stories from other parents of children with disabilities, and we feared that the doctors or nurses would treat her differently than we desired.

We felt comfortable with the Children's Hospital of Philadelphia (CHOP). They had taken care of a few of our other children through the years. We knew them and they knew us. They had treated Bella a few weeks before, and they were terrific. I sat there rocking Bella as all these thoughts went through my mind. Back and forth, back and forth, the movement soothed Bella. Karen had just given her a nebulizer treatment and chest physical therapy. Bella responded well, so Karen went down to the kitchen to make dinner. I was singing Bella lullabies, and her color was good and she was breathing easy. Eventually, the congestion returned; one moment she seemed to be fine, but in an instant it all changed and Bella's breathing became labored.

The monitor alarm blared, and I saw the monitor fall from ninety-four to eighty before I called out to Karen. She and the kids rushed in to see Bella trying to breathe, but no air was getting into her lungs. For a few seconds I tried to massage her chest and pleaded with her to keep trying to breathe, but her heart rate and oxygen levels continued to drop.

At that moment, Karen placed Bella on the changing table, assessed her, and grabbed the Ambu bag (another item we had brought home after our last visit to the hospital). She attached the oxygen tubing and began cardiopulmonary resuscitation. Karen again amazingly stabilized Bella and kept her alive until the EMTs came to continue her care. Twice in one month, Karen had been there when Bella needed her, but Bella needed both of us during the next five weeks, in three different hospitals, as we fought for the best care for her.

Perhaps Sarah Maria summed up Karen's role in taking care of Bella best. On the night Bella crashed the second time,

I had called home from the emergency room to keep the family apprised of Bella's condition. When Sarah Maria got on the phone, our precious ten-year-old, full of enthusiasm, said to me, "Dad, Mom saved Bella's life."

As I was saying, "Yes, she did," Sarah Maria continued, "and Dad, you didn't do a thing!"

The last thing I thought I would be doing in the emergency room that night was getting in a good laugh, but I think the entire floor heard me. I finally responded, "Honey, when it comes to your mom, you'll find that is the case more often than not."

8

LOVE IMPLIES SACRIFICE

• Karen Santorum •

But we have this treasure in earthen vessels, to show that the transcendent power belongs to God and not to us. We are afflicted in every way, but not crushed; perplexed, but not driven to despair; persecuted, but not forsaken; struck down, but not destroyed; always carrying in the body the death of Jesus, so that the life of Jesus may also be manifested in our bodies. For while we live we are always being given up to death for Jesus' sake, so that the life of Jesus may be manifested in our mortal flesh.

—2 CORINTHIANS 4:7–11

I watched the wipers move back and forth on the windshield. One, two. One, two. One, two. The rhythm of the slippery, squeaky sound transfixed and distracted me. The slick roads shined with silver moonlight. I shifted in my seat, stretching my arms that gripped the wheel. My body was stiff from too many nights in hospital chairs. Bella had been there for thirty-five days now. I took a sip of coffee as I wondered if the results from Bella's tests had returned. Rick would have called me if they had been bad. Or would he have waited until I got there to spare me the panic while driving? I glanced at my phone on my lap. That phone never left my side. I lived in the paradoxical fear of not hearing it ring but being afraid to pick it up because of what I might hear on the other end.

I didn't ever want to go back to all the nights when Bella was failing and on death's doorstep. The memories were too painful, so I stuffed them away, banishing them to a far corner of my mind, wanting desperately to forget. But as I drove on that road, I went back to that dark valley, to the emergency room, when stress and pain consumed me.

It was on an evening in November; I was in the kitchen, making dinner. As I chopped carrots, I recalled Bella's six-month checkup with her geneticist. He was pleasantly surprised by Bella's growth and good health. As he had said after her birth, she was writing her own book. With every filled page, there was one more reason to hope. She wasn't going to be a textbook statistic or a case number. She'd survived autumn with only one hospitalization of a few days and recovered well. With her compromised immune system, I knew how blessed we were that that was the only incident.

Our family had finally gotten into a rhythm, a new way of

living with our little Bella. The kids were doing well in school. We had found ways to juggle their after-school activities with the extra driving and the need for someone always to be home with Bella. We had prioritized simple living and looked for quality, not quantity, in our activities.

I'd even started thinking about what to cook for Thanksgiving dinner with my family. Elizabeth would do the stuffing. Sarah and the boys would help with the potatoes and vegetables. I would make the pies, and Rick would make the turkey. Some of my happiest memories with my family are of Thanksgiving morning. Now we had added a new little member to our group, one who gave us a particularly powerful reason to be thankful this year.

Bella would cheer us on from her high chair, her eyes alert and taking in all the action. Beaming, she'd kick her short, dangling legs back and forth. As always, she'd probably want to play with her plush baby doll, Gracie. Gracie wore a multicolored, patchwork dress and, like Bella, she always had a smile on her face. We'd recently discovered that Bella had a sense of humor, because whenever we laughed, Bella would join in. She was a lovable and easy audience for all the kids' bad jokes and seemed to make everything even funnier with her joyful baby squeals. If Bella was laughing, everyone couldn't help but join in.

Rick broke in on my thoughts. From upstairs, he called for me, panicked. "Karen, come quickly! Something's wrong with Bella!" I ran to our bedroom to find Rick holding Bella in the rocking chair, saying, "Something's wrong with Bella. I don't know what to do! Karen, I don't know what to do!"

My heart sank as I looked at Bella. She was quickly

spiraling downward. Lethargic. Blue lips. I listened to her heart and lungs and immediately put her on oxygen, trying to keep her oxygen saturation levels (sats) up. What had started as a simple cold just days before had moved into her lungs. Her heart-shaped face was pale, her body frail and exhausted. Her violent coughs shook her small body as she worked to clear her lungs. Within seconds, before I could start a nebulizer or chest PT, Bella went into cardiac arrest.

With monitor alarm blaring and kids screaming, "What's wrong?" I grabbed the Ambu bag, blasted the oxygen, and performed CPR. Everyone cried and screamed, trying to help me do what only I could do. Focused completely on my failing little girl, through tears I repeated, "Bella, don't go. Bella, don't go." She couldn't leave. Not in my arms. Not in front of her siblings. Not forever.

I told Elizabeth to call 911. She fumbled as she grabbed the phone and dialed. My senses were in shock. I was watching my baby die, right in front of me. I was doing everything I could, but I had no idea if it would be enough to save her. As I performed CPR, I heard Elizabeth place the call and the kids crying, asking what was happening. To this day, Elizabeth doesn't remember how she quelled her sobs long enough for the 911 operator to understand what she was saying. After she provided our address, she pleaded, "She's dying. Hurry! She's dying."

We all felt so helpless, so hopelessly and painfully inadequate. To this day, I wish I had sent my children out of the room. I wish I had protected their tender hearts. I wish they had never seen me sobbing as I was resuscitating my baby, their sister. Nothing can prepare you for such a heartbreaking and chaotic moment. I finally had the sense to ask Rick to usher the children out of the room; unfortunately, it was too late. The image of their sister walking the veil between heaven and earth is forever seared in their minds.

It felt like an eternity, but Bella responded within a few minutes. Her pink cheeks returned, heart rate normal and sats back to the high nineties. I embraced her, weeping and rocking back and forth as I sat on the bed. The paramedics arrived and took her from my shaking hands. Clad in dark uniforms and sturdy boots, their huge frames hovered over my tiny baby, making her seem even smaller than she was. They attached several cords to her body, moving swiftly and surely. The paramedic checking her vitals had coarse, large hands, but he moved with the precision and gentleness of a surgeon. I watched, fixated, still in shock. Elizabeth handed me a bag full of things for Rick, Bella, and me.

As they put Bella on the gurney, Rick and I hugged all our children, told them we loved them, and assured them that Bella would be all right. My friend Susie was on her way with a few of her children who were my kids' best friends. Bridget had just arrived. Elizabeth had called both of them. When they heard her voice, they needed no explanation. They simply said, "We're coming." Rick and I left, knowing our kids at home were in good hands.

In the back of the ambulance, I stroked Bella's curls and clung to my seat with my other hand. Her eyes were closed, the pediatric oxygen mask covering most of her pale face. They had attached sensors to her body and inserted an IV into her arm. Was this real? Just days ago she was smiling and healthy. I put my finger under her hand. But she didn't grab it. Her fingers were limp and unresponsive. I wanted to cry out, to beg her to hold it, to not let go. I needed a lifeline to throw out to her, even if it was just my hand, because I felt she was drifting away.

Listening to the sirens wail, my mind began racing with the possible outcomes. They were taking her to our local hospital, in spite of my requests to take her to a hospital that offered specialized pediatric care. Legally, they had to take her to the closest one. Looking out the back window, I saw Rick following in the car behind. The EMTs radioed the hospital to prepare the doctors. "Six-month-old infant with Trisomy 18. Went into cardiac arrest. Mother resuscitated her before our arrival. Pulmonary congestion and difficulty breathing." As they continued by reading her vitals, I felt as if I were in a nightmare. My six-month-old had just had a heart attack and could have one again if we didn't get there soon. In my head, I repeated, *Be with her. Be with her, Lord. Please.* I didn't know how else to pray in those moments.

The hospital doors burst open. A team of several doctors and nurses waited for us. Wheeling her into a room, they rushed around her, examining her and setting up the monitors. The anesthesiologist informed me that they did not have a pediatric-sized intubation tube, which was exactly my fear with going to this hospital; but he had another idea. He was able to ventilate Bella by inserting a laryngeal mask airway (LMA) instead. It was a temporary solution, and it worked. They asked me questions. Then they repeated them. Was I unclear? I didn't know. What I did know was that I had to focus. She had to get to the Children's Hospital in Philadelphia. I had to fight for my little girl. The claws came out, as did my tenacity.

Several minutes later, Rick came into the room as I was asking the doctor for a transport to CHOP, the children's hospital that we knew, loved, and trusted. I had called them directly, and they had a helicopter standing by to life flight her as soon as we gave the go-ahead. Then Rick interrupted. "I don't want to wait for a helicopter from Philadelphia to get here. It's going to take too long and it costs a lot of money."

The doctor responded, "We could transfer her to a closer hospital that can have a helicopter out here in a fraction of the time."

I didn't want to take her there. Bella's doctors, the ones she needed right then, were in Philadelphia, and CHOP offered the best medical care we could give her. We went back and forth, but Rick was resolved and told the attending physician to organize a transport to the area hospital. I didn't agree.

When Rick was a United States senator, I trusted him with the work he did; how he navigated his way through Congress and the labyrinth of the government was his area of expertise, not mine. Now it was time for him to trust me. I was raised in a medical family. My father was a physician, and seven of my siblings are physicians, nurses, and dentists. I was practically raised in a hospital, and I am a nurse who understands medicine, how to navigate through a hospital, and more specifically, the needs of critically ill infants. This was my area of expertise, and I needed my husband to trust me.

I insisted that not all hospitals are alike and there are huge differences in the quality of the education and knowledge levels of the doctors and nurses. Their skills vary widely, as well as the available medical equipment, supplies, and procedures; unfortunately, by not going to CHOP, we were taking our chances. This was not a risk I was willing to take. Not with my Bella, not with any of my children.

Two hours later, the helicopter had not arrived. We were told they should have taken about thirty minutes but were inexplicably delayed. As I paced by the window, I thought about how we could have been on our way to CHOP by now. I looked at Rick. He was on his phone. I stopped. I think he could sense my eyes boring a hole into his head, because he looked up. "This is insane." He nodded, calmly. How could he be calm at a time like this?

Just as I was about to burst with frustration, the door opened. The chopper had arrived. Their team came into the room with the attending physician. After examining her, the EMT turned to us. "We weren't aware that she had an LMA. We can't transport her with this."

My blood was boiling. I couldn't believe it. "I don't understand. You were apprised of her situation. You knew that she had this airway!"

He shuffled awkwardly, stammering to reply as he flipped through papers on his clipboard. "There was a miscommunication."

My gaze turned stony and my jaw set. Barely able to speak, I said, "Your miscommunication may cost my little girl her life!" Filled with regret and frustration, I focused on transporting Bella to a hospital that could give her proper care. Rick and I once again found ourselves in a heated discussion about where to go, and the tension overwhelmed me. I wanted to rush to CHOP, but we were promised by a hospital I no longer trusted that they would have an ambulance there right away. Rick insisted on the ambulance.

We waited for almost three more hours for the ambulance. Like a caged animal, I circled the room again and again praying for my Bella, unable to focus on anything. They arrived with no explanation as to why it took so long, and as they loaded her into the back of the ambulance, I moved to climb in with her. An EMT stopped me, "I'm sorry, but you're not allowed to ride in the ambulance with her. It's hospital policy."

I wasn't about to leave my little girl alone in an ambulance! But the EMT wouldn't budge. I had no other choice but to ride up front with the driver, away from my Bella. Rick pulled the car around and watched the ambulance drive away, and he followed. I was suffocating in a nightmare and could not break out of it.

After Bella was admitted to the pediatric intensive care unit, she was placed in a shared room. A man in uniform stood at the foot of the other bed. He stood with arms folded, feet spread wide, and stared intently at the bed in front of him. What was an armed guard doing in here? I asked the nurse, and she told me it was to keep the other patients safe. I asked her why my baby was in this room. Then, from that bed, hidden only by a flimsy curtain partition, I heard the sounds of violent vomiting.

I gasped and looked at Rick. Before either of us could say anything, alarms went off and two nurses ran into the room. They pushed back the curtain just enough for us to see that the bed was occupied by a teenage boy who was throwing up all over his bed. I wanted to wheel Bella out of the room at that very minute. I rounded Bella's bed to talk to Rick and spied a pile of soiled linens at the foot of Bella's bed. Shocked, I realized they were undoubtedly from the neighboring bed. A deathly ill baby with a seriously compromised immune system could not room with a violently ill teenager who could expose her to who knows what!

I pulled Rick out of the room. "I'm going to the head nurse to get Bella transferred to a different room."

He put his hands on my arms and said, "Calm down, Karen!"

Bad move. I shook his hands off and backed away, shaking my head in disbelief. Hurt. Angry. No, I wouldn't "calm down." My husband was always a feisty, strong, and passionate defender when the occasion arose. Who was this mellow guy? I needed the fighter, to fight with me and for our child. My body went numb. The isolation I felt sent chills through me as I turned abruptly and headed toward the nurses' station.

"We don't have any other rooms available." The nurse turned her attention back to filling out paperwork.

No rooms, huh? I walked down the hallway and rounded the PICU. Several empty rooms. Back at the nurses' station, I calmly said, "I think there must be a miscommunication, because there are several empty rooms here. My child has a seriously compromised immune system, is critically ill, and is currently in the same room with a vomiting juvenile. If you don't transfer her to a proper room, I will immediately call Children's Hospital in Philadelphia and arrange to transport her there."

The nurse stammered out an apology, remarking that they were very busy. She would see what they could do.

Thirty minutes later we were transferred to a room in another area of the PICU. This room was also shared, but at least there were no signs of vomit. The doctors came in and told us the results of the first round of bloodwork. Bella's carbon dioxide levels were through the roof, which was caused by her ineffective breathing, specifically, the fact that she wasn't exhaling fully. This buildup of carbon dioxide changed the pH in her blood, giving her metabolic acidosis, which changed the rhythm of her heart, causing a heart attack. Currently, she was on a ventilator and had what they suspected was viral *and* bacterial pneumonia in both lungs. They put together a hefty cocktail of various drugs and scheduled more tests with the hope of getting more answers.

Now into the wee hours of the morning, Rick and I were exhausted. Sitting in a chair, Rick fell asleep on the other side of Bella's bed, phone in hand. His head bobbed up and down as he dozed. Occasionally, he awakened with a jerk, looked around, and then closed his eyes again. In a chair on the other side, I felt there was much more than a twin-sized hospital bed between us. I felt very alone, as if I were the only one who was in the ring for Bella. And worse, I'd been gut punched and I was down for the count. One. Two. Three. I needed Rick to lift me up, to help me protect her.

I crossed my arms on her bed and leaned my head on them. She was asleep now. They'd given her something to help with the pain and so she could rest. Her little hands were balled into fists, pointer finger and pinkie touching. I loved those tiny hands. She looked lost in the yellow hospital gown they had put on her. Even though we had surrounded her with the proper pillows to support her, she barely took up any space on her hospital bed. Her eyelashes fluttered and she shifted her head. I wondered what she was dreaming about.

I jolted awake to the sound of bloodcurdling screams. Rick had jumped up, tense and bewildered. The child in the bed next to us was writhing in pain and screaming like I had never heard anyone scream before. Bella started wailing and cough-ing. Monitor alarms screeched as the other child's parents talked loudly in a language I didn't recognize. I stood up and started stroking Bella's head, holding her hand and talking to her. She continued to cry, but the coughing subsided. Doctors and nurses came and tended to the other child as the scream-ing continued. After hours of nearly constant screaming, I asked the nurse once again if we could be placed somewhere else. We were striking out again and again.

In the days that followed, Rick and I took turns keeping vigil at Bella's bedside. We became like two shadows, passing each other in fluorescent-lit halls. Thanksgiving came and went. The dream of preparing the great meal with my fam-ily: gone. Not being together as a family on Thanksgiving was sad and unnatural. I was home with the children for breakfast, and Rick for dinner. Bridget spent Thanksgiving away from her family to be with us. I don't know what I would have done without her. She managed the house, took care of the kids, and became a source of strength and support for them. She and Elizabeth did all the cooking that Thanksgiving. We all did our best, prayed together, and counted our blessings.

◆　　◆　　◆

After six months, Rick was still stoic. He kept it together and was "at peace." As much as it pained me, I learned what that meant to him. He was at peace if Bella lived or died. And that broke my heart. We both abandoned ourselves to Divine Providence, but I believe we understood that term very differ-ently. I came to accept Bella's diagnosis while simultaneously deepening my trust in the Lord, but that didn't mean I wasn't going to fight for her. Trust did not mean abandoning her. Rick accepted who Bella was from the very beginning. I loved his acceptance of Bella and I drew strength from it. But as the first six months of Bella's life passed, I think Rick resigned himself too wholly to the fate many doctors and statistics had predicted for her. He thought I was fighting a fight we couldn't win.

We were at a hospital that treated our baby girl like an "it" rather than a person worthy of dignity and respect. About a week after Bella had been in the hospital, the attending doctor said he needed to talk. I'll call him Dr. Grim. He informed me that he would no longer be taking Bella's arterial blood gases (ABGs). As a nurse, I knew that if a critically ill patient, like Bella, was on a ventilator, ABGs were crucial to monitoring oxygen and carbon dioxide levels, as well as pH and other essential blood concentrations. The ABGs were also a guide for adjusting the ventilator parameters.

Surprised, I asked Dr. Grim why he was doing that. Never referring to Bella by name, he gave me an explanation that made no sense at all. I stood there looking at him as he tapped his clipboard with his fingers, wondering how many parents of special-needs children he had fooled, and asked, "Since when do we take IQ tests to determine a patient's level of care?" His eyes glazed over me and eventually he admitted that his decision was a means of cost containment. I told him that he was in the wrong profession and should have been an accountant. That was the last straw. Having a baby in the PICU was extremely stressful, but being in this particular hospital added another layer of stress that was wide as the ocean and almost crushing.

Equally disturbing was the fact that Dr. Grim never did a head-to-toe, hands-on assessment of Bella. Rick and I were taking shifts at the hospital and had just assumed that Bella was being checked when the other person was there with her. In our exhaustion we missed something that is crucially important for our Bella, or for any patient in the hospital, especially the PICU. This moment was a shocking revelation for us.

I called CHOP immediately to organize a transport for Bella. Typically, there's a chain of command to follow in order to organize a transport, but I wanted to be involved to ensure she was transported immediately. I knew if we waited for Dr. Grim to arrange the transfer, it was not going to happen. Weeping and barely able to speak, I asked the transport team at CHOP to come and get Bella even though transports are never arranged this way. I also spoke with the head nurse at CHOP's PICU and asked for a bed for Bella. The team at CHOP worked with the staffers at the area hospital and arranged for an ambulance to pick her up. CHOP physicians and nurses would never say anything negative about another hospital, but they heard a crying, desperate mother on the other end of the phone, begging them to come and get Bella. The CHOP transport team could not get there soon enough.

After the transport had been arranged, Dr. Grim came into Bella's room to apologize and admitted that he never should have suggested withdrawing the ABG tests and he should have been more involved with Bella's care. I stood there in silence as the tears rolled down my face, thinking about the prayer I prayed every day, the Our Father: ". . . Give us this day our daily bread, and forgive us our trespasses *as we forgive those who trespass against us* . . ." After a few moments I told him that I forgave him and would pray that he would think about that with his next special-needs patient.

When the CHOP transport team walked through the door of Bella's room, I breathed a huge sigh of relief. Momma Bear could finally get off her hind legs and pull in her claws. They came to care for Bella, but they rescued me too. After a smooth transport, we arrived at CHOP. I was comforted knowing that Bella was in such an exceptional place with an outstanding team. I looked at my sweet little girl and knew she was in the best hands. The stress melted away, and finally I could get some rest. The physicians, nurses, and therapists who cared for Bella were all bright and compassionate. Finally, my Bella was getting the care she deserved.

Several days after she'd been at CHOP, I remember looking at her small body attached to more tubes and wires than I could count. Her cheeks were swollen from the steroids, her body frail from exhaustion, and her eyes glazed and out of focus. But the whole time, Bella had hardly cried. I tucked her pink blankets in around her and she turned to look at me. "I love you, sweetheart." The sound of my voice made her eyes light up. She looked up at my face, and she smiled for the first time since she'd been admitted to the hospital.

After Bella arrived at CHOP, Rick and I started overlapping our days so we could have time together. It was a healing time as we spent hours talking, praying, watching movies, and holding each other. It felt so good to be together and reconnect after such a stressful time. We loved our time with each other and were very involved with Bella's care. When Rick was there, I would take breaks and walk through the hospital.

Exercise has always been my stress relief. Some people think that being a mom is enough to give you gray hairs, but as a nurse, worries were always added as I repeatedly diagnosed my children in my head with serious illnesses they did not have. If they had a headache, I worried they had a brain tumor. If they had a cough, I worried it was tuberculosis. My fears created a toxic mix of concern. I needed an outlet, and so I walked. Up and down the hallways where hope lived, I walked and soon realized that the pro-life fight is also being fought at the bedsides of these very special kids. The fight doesn't end at birth, but continues on with infants born with birth defects, whose lives are too often judged as not worth living.

The weeks came and went. Christmas was fast approaching. As I traveled the streets of Philadelphia, I watched the bright lights, wreaths, and cheery decorations take their places in shop windows and on streetlamps. Christmas music played softly everywhere I went, but it felt like a soundtrack to another life, one lived outside of hospital walls. In mid-December, Rick arrived in Philadelphia and, once again, we switched places. I returned home after a long few days at the hospital.

After a three-hour drive, I pulled into the driveway, exhausted. Then, looking at the house, I was astonished. The front of the house was all lit up. The bushes twinkled, wreaths hung on the doors, and candles glowed in the windows. Getting out of the car, I took it all in, smelling the homey scent of pine and burning firewood. The front door opened and the kids came running out. "Surprise, Mommy!" Standing in the front yard, they hugged me as we enjoyed the scene. Taking my hand, they led me inside. "Close your eyes, Mom. . . . Okay, now you can open them!"

The children had worked hard to create a Christmas wonderland. The tree was up, the stockings hung, and every corner of the house held our family's Christmas treasures. The boys stoked a roaring, cozy fire in the family room, and the girls simmered hot chocolate on the stove next to, my favorite, chocolate chip cookies. We sat together, reading Christmas stories and talking. The kids knew my heart needed to be home with them. I treasure my children and love them with all my heart. Their sweet gestures filled me with warmth and comfort. An oasis.

During those special days at home, Elizabeth told me a story about a game she and Bridget had played with the other kids. Bridget got the idea from a family friend who had suffered loss. This friend had used the game to encourage her own kids to feel comfortable talking about their feelings during a difficult time. So, Bridget and Elizabeth played it with our children.

They wrote out a list of twelve questions. Some were silly and some were more serious, but the point was to get the kids talking. They rolled two dice, and whatever number they got, they'd have to answer the corresponding question. As they went around the circle, they talked about their favorite family memories, what they wanted for Christmas, and a whole host of other topics.

Then it was our seven-year-old Patrick's turn. When he rolled the dice, he got this question: "How did you feel the night Bella went to the hospital?" The children were quiet as they waited for his response. "It was so loud and I was so scared," he answered. "Then I thought about a lot of things. I know that Bella's an angel and that angels have to go to heaven, but I just don't want her to go yet." His lips trembled and he looked at the floor, reaching for Elizabeth's hand. They all agreed they couldn't have said it better themselves.

A week before Christmas, Rick and I brought Sarah, Peter, and Patrick up to Philadelphia to visit Bella, and also to have fun. Between visits with their sister, I took them to Independence National Historic Park, the Children's Museum, and, of course, out for the famous Philly cheesesteak sandwiches. We thoroughly enjoyed this time together. They learned a great deal of history and we had plenty of fun.

On one of our visits to the hospital, as they colored pictures for Bella by her hospital bed, I walked over to the window. It was snowing. Watching the large, fuzzy flakes drifting slowly through the cold night air, I conjured memories of all my little ones bundled in their snowsuits and hats, running through the snow, catching snowflakes on their tongues. My children loved the snow, and some of our best memories are sledding and building igloos together.

I was lost in memories, and drifting away from the hospital for a little while felt good. The kids joined me at the window, mesmerized by the beautiful sight as Bella drifted off to sleep. Looking up at me, they asked, "Can we go make snow angels?" I smiled and grabbed their coats. We tiptoed around the room so as not to wake Bella, and kissed Rick. They crept out of the room, but I paused before leaving to make sure Bella had not awakened. Sarah had put a pink bow in Bella's dark hair. Her cheeks were rosy, her lips rounded into an *o* as she slept. In her hospital bed, she looked like our own little snow angel.

Crossing the street, we walked to a nearby park. The kids ran around, laughing and stomping on the freshly fallen snow. Winter was here and Christmas was around the corner.

•　　•　　•

Bella was at CHOP for several weeks. Her recovery had many ups and downs, but CHOP's medical pioneers and their cutting-edge treatments ultimately saved Bella's life. The pneumonia cleared up, and Bella got off the ventilator. Words cannot express our gratitude for the exceptional care she received. Dr. Blinman and Robin Cook visited us nearly every day, offering compassion, friendship, and guidance. Their visits and the joy they always brought into Bella's hospital room helped us more than words can say. We love them both.

The physicians, nurses, and therapists took excellent care of Bella. They were friendly and addressed Bella by name, included Rick and me with rounds every morning, allowed our children to visit and stay overnight, and even had a stocked kitchen for the parents to use. These sound like little amenities, but they were huge. We were shut out from rounds at the other hospital, but the physicians at CHOP wanted our input every day. At CHOP, my Bella was a person, a beautiful baby girl who was loved and treated with the ultimate dignity and respect. CHOP's motto is "Where Hope Lives," and the physicians often said, "Just give her a chance."

After nearly six weeks, Bella was cleared to go home a few days before Christmas. Rick and I took down the many cards, signs, and drawings we had taped to her hospital walls. Crayon drawings of princesses, "get well" wishes, and marker-swirled pages drawn by the children were placed carefully into a plastic bag. We packed Bella's blankets and toys. Many people had visited, sent flowers and cards, and offered support. Back home again, we received a constant supply of homemade meals from our circle of friends. A strong prayer chain strengthened and sustained us. Our families and friends were the hands of Christ during her hospitalization.

Bella came home to the open arms of her siblings and a cozy home that was decorated for her first Christmas. Christmas is a season of light and birth, a joyful time of remembrance, gratitude, and celebration. That Christmas, we thanked God for the gift of His newborn Son, but also for the gift of our own little babe. He had given her back to us. We went to separate Masses on Christmas Eve so that both Rick and I could also stay home with Bella. She was still fragile and needed rest and oxygen. But that evening, with a little help from us, Bella was able to place baby Jesus in the manger. Singing "Silent Night," we watched this special moment and offered prayers of thanksgiving.

On Christmas morning, the kids raced back to our room. "Wake up! It's Christmas!" They were beckoning to Bella. They crowded around her crib, watching her stretch and coo as she awakened. Sarah and Elizabeth took charge of carefully dressing their little baby doll in her red satin Christmas dress, white tights, Mary Janes, and a red bow. After opening presents and enjoying breakfast, Rick and I placed a special phone call to the family of Bella's spiritual brother, Brendan.

◆　◆　◆

In 2000, Rick and I had been blessed to meet Pope John Paul II in Rome. It was our fourth visit with our spiritual father who we loved with all our hearts. At the time, a three-year-old boy in our community, Brendan Kelly, was battling a virulent form of leukemia, so we brought his picture with us to give to the pope and asked him to pray for Brendan. The next year, Brendan was in remission and was granted a wish by the Make-A-Wish

Foundation. His wish was to meet the man who had prayed for him in Rome.

Brendan's struggles with leukemia and the debilitating treatments had been an inspiration to all who knew him. But it wasn't until Bella was born that we fully understood how very special he was. When Brendan found out about Bella's condition, he committed to pray for her daily. They became spiritual friends because Bella was born with Trisomy 18 and Brendan with Trisomy 21, or Down syndrome.

During the weeks Bella was in the hospital, Brendan was receiving chemotherapy for a relapse of leukemia. Getting a ten-year-old to take medicine that makes him violently ill is not easy, but during that time Brendan would courageously swallow the pills or take the injection and offer up his suffering as a plea to Jesus to heal Bella. Frank, his father, told me that when the pain was the worst, Brendan would repeatedly groan, "I love you, Bella." Amazing.

On that Christmas morning, we called Brendan to thank him and to wish the Kellys a Merry Christmas. We learned that Brendan had a special Christmas wish. He wanted to meet "his Bella." Frank and Maura, who were a great source of comfort and strength to us, brought their Brendan over, and the two spiritual friends met for the first time. Sitting on the couch next to the Christmas tree, Brendan received Bella into his arms. Both of their faces were swollen from steroids, pale from too many days inside hospital walls, but beautifully peaceful. Brendan kissed Bella's forehead again and again, saying, "I love you, my baby Bella."

Bella looked at him intently and sweetly, as if to say, "Oh, there you are."

Hugging her closely, he placed his head against hers and closed his eyes tightly as happy tears escaped down his face. It was one of the sweetest things we've ever seen.

Brendan and Bella reminded us that love not only implies sacrifice, but that true and unselfish love is in itself an act of sacrifice. They bore their painful treatments and sick days with joy, lifting us up through their hope and happiness. Brendan often spoke of sacrifice, of offering up his own sufferings so that Bella would be well. I like to think that, even in her peaceful silence, Bella did the same for Brendan.

9

LOVE OBLIGATES KNOWLEDGE OF THE BELOVED

• *Karen Santorum* •

[T]hou didst form my inward parts,
thou didst knit me together in my mother's womb.
I praise thee, for thou art fearful and wonderful.
Wonderful are thy works!
Thou knowest me right well.

—PSALM 139:13–14

I t was a rainy, cold winter morning. The snow that had fallen a few days before, outlining the shrubs and trees in white and making the world look magical, was melting. The world around us went from looking peaceful and pure to dreary and dark. It was the kind of day when you want to pull the blankets up and stay in bed when the alarm goes off. The aroma of freshly brewed coffee filled the air, and a cup of hot coffee on this cold morning was just what I needed.

I dragged myself out of bed after being up with Bella several times through the night and got Sarah, Peter, and Patrick off to school. We talked at breakfast about their school day and after-school sports schedules and were all laughing because Patrick told us a funny joke. When we realized it was 7:10 and they should have left at 7:00, they ran out the door with their backpacks and lunch boxes, but I managed to fit in hugs and "I love you" three times.

Every morning when the children leave for school, I light a candle and say my morning prayers. I thank God for watching over us during the night, offer up special intentions, thank Him for the gift of this new day, and ask Him to bless and protect my family. As I was reading a meditation, my eyes got heavy, and before I knew it I was asleep at the table. I was awakened to Bella's singing on the baby monitor. It's a two-way video monitor, so I pushed the button and said, "Good morning, beautiful!" With that, Bella was beaming with smiles as always.

I stood up from the table, half awake, closed my robe to keep the chill out, and went up to hold Bella. She loves listening to music in the morning, especially Enya, Disney, and Celtic Women. We snuggled in bed as we talked about the day and sang a few songs. It reminded me of all the times Rick and I would wake up in the morning to our six other children who, when they were small, would wander back into our room and nestle into our arms. Eventually, I had to break away from my morning Bella bliss to begin the work of the day. When I'm with Bella, time seems to stand still and my worries melt away.

◆　　◆　　◆

Rick was away, unfortunately. I say "unfortunately" because I missed him so much, but also because he actually enjoys grocery shopping, and we needed some groceries. When Rick shops, he uses coupons and compares the prices of every item before putting something into the cart. He does not brand-name shop; rather, he buys the least expensive items. He can tell you the price of everything in the cart and how much money he saved; sadly, I cannot say the same.

When I shop, it's always my goal to get through the store as quickly as possible, so I put all the items on my list into the cart in minutes, and off I go. Maybe it's because for almost twenty-four years I always had a baby, toddler, little kid, or big kid with me. Sometimes it was one, and other times I would be shopping with several of my children. The only pause was in the produce section, where I really enjoy teaching my children how to pick out the best fresh fruits and vegetables.

Bridget was brushing Bella's hair, and I gave my little sweetie a kiss and left for the grocery store. The cold air managed to make its way through my winter coat and the double layer of insulated clothing as I scraped the ice and heavy wet snow off our truck. We had not had a garage for seven and a half years, and on this particular morning a garage would have been a dream. The untouched foot of softly fallen snow was now shoveled, driven on, walked on, and rained on. It was a slushy mess, and as I drove, the white snow turned to gray and brown.

By the time I reached the grocery store, the truck had warmed up and I could no longer see my breath. I sat in the parking lot for a moment, enjoying the warmth. The parking space next to me was for people with disabilities. When Bella is with me, I use these spaces all the time; they help to be closer to the doctors' offices or stores. That disability placard was a hard thing to apply for, simply because it carried with it so many raw emotions. It was a hard moment when it came in the mail and I opened the envelope.

A woman in a minivan pulled up next to me in the disability space and put her placard on the mirror. Her boots hit the slush and she almost slipped. She kicked away as much of the snow and slush as possible, and as the side door slid open, there was a little girl in a wheelchair. She was bundled up in a pink coat and wore a pink hat that appeared to be hand knit. There were golden curls peeking out under the rim of the hat. The woman, whom I assumed was her mother, pressed something that pulled out the lift and safely brought the girl out of the van and to the ground. The little girl was smiling and sticking out her tongue as if to catch snowflakes. The mom smiled back and said, "Are you catching raindrops?" She quickly grabbed her purse and pushed her daughter into the store.

Another car pulled up into a disability space and an elderly woman got out very slowly. Maybe it was because she did not want to slip, or maybe it was hard for her to move. As she stood up, she was attempting to adjust her nasal cannula with her gloves on. Her oxygen tank hung over her shoulder, concealed in a black canvas bag. I went over to her and offered her my arm and cover under my umbrella.

She cheerfully said, "Well, good morning, sunshine! Thank you for walking with me . . . I had to come out in this rain for my prescriptions, but, oh well; I think I'll get a few things while I'm here." We picked out some apples and bananas together and talked for a little while. My habit of rushing through the store vanished, as I was intrigued by the joy of this woman who was carrying a lot of heavy burdens.

For nearly seven years, I've watched these individuals and families through the eyes of a mother with a child with disabilities. Like anything in life, you have no idea of the daily challenges until you've walked the journey yourself. I thought as a neonatal intensive care nurse that I understood their daily struggles, but I didn't know the half of it. When they pull into the disabled parking spaces, or lug their bags and medical supplies through physicians' offices and hospital corridors, or wait patiently in the waiting rooms of the doctors attending their loved ones, I watch them and think about the huge effort it took for them to get through their morning care and out the door. Details are everything, and missing one detail could mean a medical crisis. Their burdens are heavy, but I've been inspired by the resiliency and joy in the many people I've met on my journey.

We are different nationalities and religions and work in different careers and live in different neighborhoods in different parts of the world—but we are united by our children.

We have suffered the sting of a challenging diagnosis, survived doctor visits and hospital stays. We have managed to navigate a complex and confusing medical world with long waits from one answering machine to another, only to think we've received a solution once we finally reach a real person, but then realize we were led down a dead-end alley by a health insurance company—again and again.

We frequently have to demand care, even basic care, and spend countless hours researching medical issues and finding the right physicians, therapists, and health care supply companies. In addition to usual daily care, there are always therapies and exercises to do, medications to administer, and medical supplies to clean, restock, and order. We have to thrive on very little sleep and learn how to be champions with handling stress. We carry hand sanitizer in our purses, pockets, bags, and cars, and use it frequently. We have specialized radar for germs, and cringe whenever someone coughs or sneezes around our special loved one.

We are united as one with our daily frustrations, worries, cares, exhaustion, and, yes, immeasurable joy. We have learned to stand tall and be a light in the darkness, and we have learned there are blessings even during the most challenging times.

A friend of mine, who has a special-needs child, sent a story to me that I've read many times. It's sweet and has a powerful message. It was written in 1987 by Emily Perl Kingsley and is a metaphor of the differences between the excitement in having and raising a normal, healthy child and having and raising a special-needs child. Here it is:

Welcome to Holland

by Emily Perl Kingsley

I am often asked to describe the experience of raising a child with a disability—to try to help people who have not shared that unique experience to understand it, to imagine how it would feel. It's like this . . .

When you're going to have a baby, it's like planning a fabulous vacation trip to Italy. You buy a bunch of guidebooks and make your wonderful plans. The Coliseum. The Michelangelo David. The gondolas of Venice. You may learn some handy phrases in Italian. It's all very exciting.

After months of eager anticipation, the day finally arrives. You pack your bags and off you go. Several hours later, the plane lands. The flight attendant comes in and says, "Welcome to Holland!"

"Holland?" you say. "What do you mean, Holland? I signed up for Italy! I'm supposed to be in Italy. All my life I've dreamed of going to Italy." But there's been a change in the flight plan. They've landed in Holland and there you must stay. The important thing is that they haven't taken you to a horrible, disgusting, filthy place full of pestilence, famine, and disease. It's just a different place.

So you must go out and buy new guidebooks. And you must learn a whole new language. And you will meet a whole new group of people you would never have met. It's just a *different* place. It's slower paced than Italy, less flashy than Italy. But after you've been there for a while and you catch your breath, you look around . . . and you begin to notice that

Holland has windmills . . . and Holland has tulips. Holland even has Rembrandts. But everyone you know is busy coming and going from Italy . . . and they're all bragging about what a wonderful time they had there. And for the rest of your life you will say, "Yes, that's where I was supposed to go. That's what I had planned."

And the pain of that experience will never, ever, ever, ever go away . . . because the loss of that dream is a very, very significant loss. But . . . if you spend your life mourning the fact that you didn't get to Italy, you may never be free to enjoy the very special, the very lovely things . . . about Holland.

Bella was our eighth baby and our second trip to Holland. Our first trip to Holland was with our son Gabriel Michael, who was our fourth baby. He was born and died in our arms two hours after his birth, and with his death went all our hopes and dreams for his life. Through the tears I saw many beautiful things in Holland, but never ever wanted to return. We were brought back to Holland with Bella, and once again, all our hopes and dreams for her life were like fuzzy dandelions blown away in the wind. Like the metaphor of the excitement of going to Italy and seeing all the wonderful sites there, only to be disappointed at being told we were not going to the Sistine Chapel, or to the Coliseum, or to any of the magnificent sites in Italy, our plans had been changed and we were going someplace else.

The truth is that Rick and I have been to Italy six times with our other children and have enjoyed the splendor of every possible place in Italy. It's been a complete joy raising Elizabeth, John, Daniel, Sarah Maria, Peter, and Patrick. It's been a complete joy sharing with them the day to day, watching them learn and grow, cheering them on with their accomplishments, and holding them during their disappointments. We are so proud of each and every one of them, and through the years we have enjoyed the beauty and brilliance of everything Italy has to offer.

However, I would not trade going to Holland for the world. Bella is almost seven, and raising her has shown us the beauty and brilliance of everything in Holland. For it was in Holland that I learned a new language; it was in Holland that my eyes were opened to the gifts of this new land; and it was in Holland that I learned pure joy and some of the most important lessons in life.

Raising Bella has been a different experience from raising our other children. Instead of concerning myself with breast-feeding and growth charts, I was worried about my baby surviving another day. Instead of healthy pediatric visits, our schedules were filled with time-consuming visits with several specialists. Instead of taking my little girl to soccer camps and ballet lessons, we do physical therapy. Instead of buying dollhouses and tricycles, we're always looking for adaptive toys and enabling devices. Instead of running freely through spring meadows, my little girl is in her walker, taking baby steps across our kitchen floor.

Instead of homeschooling as I've done for all our other children for the past eighteen years, I homeschool Bella in a very different way. We read books and sing songs, but we also do occupational therapy, physical therapy, riding therapy, music therapy, and massage therapy. This is my new world of homeschooling, and I would not trade this time with Bella for anything in the world.

Through the years, my family has gotten to know Bella

and her cute, spunky personality and all her health issues, and what makes her happy, and what she does not like. Our dear Lord knows us and is a good example of how we, as parents, should know our children.

> *O LORD, thou hast searched me and known me!*
> *Thou knowest when I sit down and when I rise up;*
>   *thou discernest my thoughts from afar.*
> *Thou searchest out my path and my lying down,*
>   *and art acquainted with all my ways.*
> *Even before a word is on my tongue,*
>   *lo, O LORD, thou knowest it altogether.*
> *Thou dost beset me behind and before,*
>   *and layest thy hand upon me. (Ps. 139:1–5)*

For the past seven years, as with all our children, we have been getting to know our little girl. Her physicians and therapists have been great blessings in our lives. I've talked about several of them as part of our getting to know Bella and her issues. One of her biggest issues is breathing, and Dr. Lisa Elden and Dr. Suzanne Beck have used their expertise to assist us. Dr. Elden, who is an exceptional ENT (ear, nose, and throat) physician and skilled surgeon, did Bella's bronchoscopy when Bella was seven months old. This test provided valuable information about Bella's airways and gave us direction in her care. Dr. Elden also put in Bella's ear tubes that were a lifesaver whenever Bella was congested. When Bella was two and a half years old, Dr. Elden removed her adenoids, which greatly improved her breathing. Dr. Elden is kind and pleasant, and we just think the world of her. Her care of Bella was superb, and Bella did remarkably well with each procedure.

Dr. Beck is an extremely bright physician who is in charge of the Children's Hospital of Philadelphia's Sleep Lab. Through the years Bella has had a few sleep studies under the care of Dr. Beck. These studies have given us a lot of very specific and important information regarding Bella's breathing and sleeping patterns. Dr. Beck has always been thoughtful and generous with her time with us. She explains things really well and answers all our questions. Under her care, Bella has been on a BiPAP (bi-level positive airway pressure) machine for several years and has done really well. When she's on the BiPAP, Bella does not have apneas, and her oxygen levels are very good when she sleeps. Because of the BiPAP, Bella is able to get a good night's sleep and has a lot more energy throughout the day.

Francie Mitchell is Bella's physical therapist and is one of the most cheerful people I've ever known. She thoroughly enjoys her work and cares deeply about her patients. Bella loves her sessions with Francie and smiles the entire time as she's listening to her music and bouncing, stretching, reaching, and standing. Francie is a very bright and talented physical therapist, and she has been a great guide for us with learning how to keep Bella strong and healthy. She's taught us how to use all the different balls and therapy toys with Bella.

Lynne Ganz is Bella's occupational therapist, who also does cranial sacral therapy. When Bella is with her, she begins the session sitting at a small table with her braces on and her feet on the floor. Bella does fine motor activities with a lot of different toys. Lynne is very patient and encouraging. When Bella shows signs that she's had enough, we lay her on a table and Lynne does cranial sacral therapy, which always relaxes Bella. How I would love to have a few of those sessions myself!

When Bella was at the Children's Hospital of Philadelphia, the therapists there worked with her and taught Rick and me how to do the varying therapies. There's no doubt in my mind that part of the reason Bella has done so well is because of these therapies. From the time Bella was a baby in the NICU, she has loved having her tiny feet massaged. My dear sister Sue called me one day and recommended that we do foot massages. For nearly seven years, Bella has had her feet massaged with lavender oil while listening to the sounds of whales in the ocean!

When we bathe her, she also gets a full-body massage. I had always done infant massage with my babies, but I learned so much more at CHOP about techniques and the benefits of massage. There was also a speech therapist at CHOP who worked closely with us, helping Bella with her feedings.

After navigating the storms of the first year of Bella's life, she got much stronger with each passing year. My dear sister Kathy and her husband, Mike, were a constant source of help and guidance for us. They are both physicians, and their medical advice helped us through some tough times. We call Mike "Dr. House," because he's brilliant and will never stop researching and putting all the pieces of a personal medical profile together, as puzzling as it may be, until he's figured out a solution. It was Mike who sent Rick and me articles from the medical journals after Bella's birth about the infants in Japan with Trisomy 18 who were doing well. He told us not to give up on Bella.

When Bella was three, I received a call from Mike. He asked if we had ever had Bella's IgG (immunoglobulin) subclass levels checked. I told him that when Bella was seven months old, her IgG levels were checked, but not the subclass levels. He had, once again, taken the time to do some research on children with Trisomy 18 and discovered they tend to have low immunoglobulin subclass levels.

Immunoglobulins, also known as antibodies, are an important part of our immune system; they neutralize bacteria and viruses. They are divided into a number of classes and subclasses that are found in different areas of the body, each having a unique biological function. Our immunoglobulins play several roles in fighting infections, and if any of the levels are low, a person can have repeat infections. This research would end up being crucial for our Bella.

◆ ◆ ◆

After Bella's first year, she was stronger, and we settled into a new life with her. Bella was a happy baby girl, and our family doted on her. She was constantly held and cared for and loved. Unfortunately, she got several respiratory infections every year, including a few confirmed cases of pneumonia. It seemed as though we would get through one infection and soon after, despite our hand washing, clean home, and keeping her away from anyone who was sick, she would be sick again.

When Bella got sick, she would decline and go into what we called a *death spiral*. Her illnesses always started with a runny nose that spread to her lungs within a few days, no matter how much suctioning and how many treatments we were doing. She would take shallow breaths, have apneas, and not ventilate properly. She would get tachycardic, and together, Rick and I would somehow manage to get through the long, stressful, emotional, and sleepless nights. The worry made me feel as though I aged twenty years every time Bella was sick, and it was during these times that I would pray constantly:

> *For thou didst form my inward parts,*
> *thou didst knit me together in my mother's womb.*
> *I praise thee, for thou art fearful and wonderful.*
> *Wonderful are thy works!*
> *Thou knowest me right well;*
> *my frame was not hidden from thee,*
> *when I was being made in secret,*
> *intricately wrought in the depths of the earth.*
> *Thy eyes beheld my unformed substance;*
> *in thy book were written, every one of them,*
> *the days that were formed for me,*
> *when as yet there was none of them.*
> *How precious to me are thy thoughts, O God!*
>
> (Ps. 139:13–17)

Together, Rick and I would pray and ask our Lord to hold Bella in His loving arms and heal her. God made her in His image, and He knows everything about her. Bella is wonderfully made! In those long sleepless nights, I could feel Christ's presence. He was there guiding and comforting us, and He always healed His little angel. It was remarkable that even in sickness in the middle of the night as the moon shed its light through Bella's window, she would look up at us, beaming with smiles as if she were an angel.

We made many trips to our local pulmonologist office in Bella's first few years of life. The physicians there were smart, thoughtful, and kind. They always did a complete medical assessment with Bella and listened carefully to her lungs, and they were attentive to her and responsive with ordering her medications. The nurses responded to my calls right away and were very helpful. This established pattern of repeat infections, however, was a red flag that something might be off with her immunoglobulins.

I like to think it was just an oversight, and not because of Bella's diagnosis, that a simple blood test to check her immunoglobulin levels had not been ordered. Whatever the reason, I forgive them and know that we are all human and make mistakes; in addition, I understand that there's still so much to learn in medicine. Thankfully, my brother-in-law, Mike, took the time to research this issue and urged me to have Bella's levels checked. He wrote a letter to Bella's pediatrician and pulmonologist discussing the studies he had found. I talked with our pediatrician about it, and he appreciated the information and ordered the test.

The results of Bella's blood test confirmed that she did have a severe deficiency with both her main immunoglobulin levels and also one of her subclass levels. Rick and I immediately took Bella to the immunology department at the Children's Hospital of Philadelphia. As always, the CHOP physicians could not have been more wonderful. Bella saw Dr. Jen Heimall and Dr. Kathleen Sullivan. They did a thoughtful and thorough exam and ordered another blood test. We talked at length about immunotherapy and its benefits and drawbacks. After several discussions we decided that, given Bella's pattern of repeat serious infections with bronchitis and pneumonia, she would benefit from immunotherapy.

Bella received the first infusion up at CHOP, and they

taught Rick and me how to administer it. The infusion is given through a very small subcutaneous needle, not an IV, so I give it to Bella once a week. For three years I've been giving Bella her Hizentra (immunoglobulin) therapy here at home, and it has completely changed her life! Bella got off all her daily medications and treatments. She went from being a little girl who was frequently sick and congested to being consistently healthy and able to breathe well. Because she could breathe well, she began sleeping through the night and had a lot more energy during the day.

Her occupational and physical therapists noticed a big difference in Bella's energy levels during her therapy sessions, and as a result she's progressing much better with her fine and gross motor skills. The Hizentra immunoglobulin therapy has made literally a night and day difference in Bella's life! We are rarely at the doctor's office anymore. When Bella does get sick, instead of doing her death spiral, she gets better quickly. It's amazing the difference in my little girl. Rick and I will always be so grateful to Dr. Mike Lamb for taking the time to care and to the physicians at CHOP for taking such great care of Bella!

The difference in Bella's life and the life of my entire family is so huge and significant with the immunoglobulin therapy. Any child who presents with frequent infections and establishes a pattern of sickness is evaluated for numerous things. When different medications and treatments are tried but are ineffective in preventing future illnesses, eventually a patient's immunoglobulin levels should be checked. It might just be a lifesaver.

Bella

Our beautiful angel on earth

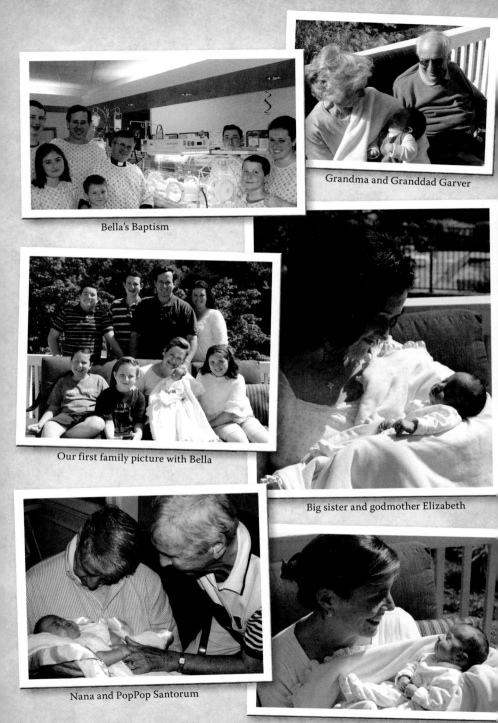

Bella's Baptism

Grandma and Granddad Garver

Our first family picture with Bella

Big sister and godmother Elizabeth

Nana and PopPop Santorum

Susie and Bella

Patrick and Bella

Peter and Bella

Katy at Bella's first birthday party with Karen and Rick.

Friends at Bella's first birthday

Bella playing cards with Peter and Patrick

Bella with Karen on her first birthday

Bella reading a book with Sarah Maria

Bella loves playing with her
brothers and sisters

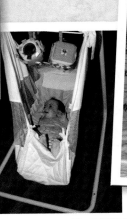

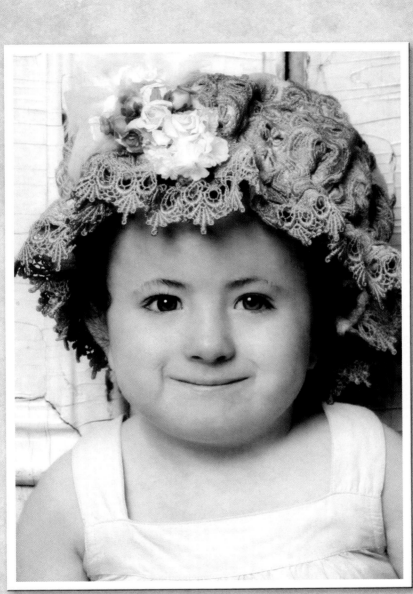

Photos courtesy of "Timeless Portraits by Liz," Sewickley, PA

Sarah Maria, Patrick and
Peter welcome Bella home
from the hospital.

Proud big brother John
experiencing the joy
of holding Bella

Bella's special friend Brendan

Bella celebrates her second Christmas

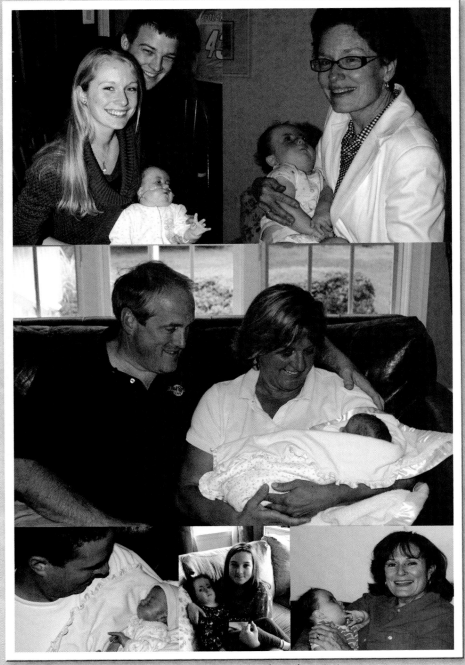

Bella is loved by her aunts, uncles and cousins!

Photos courtesy of "Timeless Portraits by Liz," Sewickley, PA

Bella's third birthday

Proud big brother Daniel with Bella

Rick and Bella

Bella Donna Chapel Fresco

Christmas 2010

Bella taking a bike ride with Rick, Karen, Peter, and Patrick

Bella taking a walk with Sarah Maria, Peter, Karen and Daniel

Bella swimming in the pool

Bella fishing with the boys

Bella at the beach, playing the piano with Elizabeth, on a tractor ride and reading with Patrick

John and Bella

Bridget and Bella

Elizabeth
and Bella

Family with Bridget and Steven

Sarah Maria and Bella

Leanne and Mark (godfather)
Bella's fifth birthday

Loved by so many!

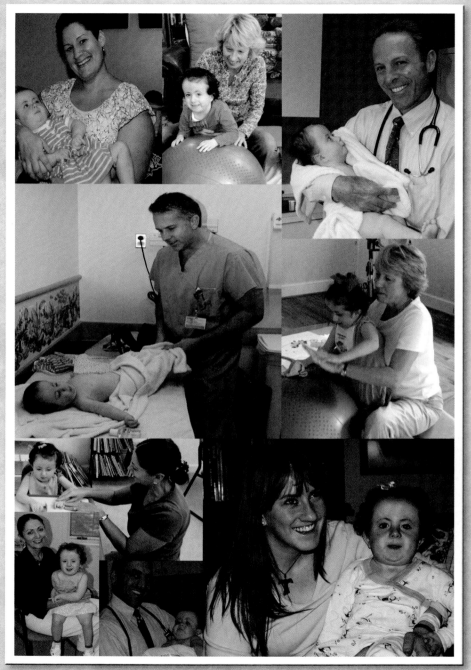

Bella's Exceptional Caregivers

Bella with Grandma and
Granddad Garver

The family with Nana and Pop Pop Santorum

The Santorums with Grandma Garver. Easter 2014

SUGAR AND SPICE AND EVERYTHING NICE,
THAT'S WHAT LITTLE BELLA IS MADE OF.

10

LOVE IS UNCONDITIONAL

• Rick Santorum •

[T]he Lord appeared to him from afar.
I have loved you with an everlasting love;
therefore I have continued my faithfulness to you.

—JEREMIAH 31:3

A few years back, I was having lunch to catch up on the life of a young man who was on my staff when I was a US senator. When the conversation turned to his marriage, he said, "I am not getting what I want out of my marriage." I responded, "Good!"

My reaction startled him, so I went on to explain that marriage is a sacrificial relationship of giving yourself to your spouse, not a business contract for a delivery of needed goods and services. His understanding of marriage is widely accepted and often the reason for the high divorce rate. Today, marriage is all about "what I get," and not about "what I can give" to my spouse and our marriage.

I know a man who is on his fifth marriage. He sums up the contemporary view of marriage rather bluntly, "If my marriage contract isn't performing, then I cancel the contract and find another partner to marry." To him, marriage is about romance, pleasure, and companionship. All very important aspects of marriage, but like any contract it is not just about what you receive; it's what you give, like commitment, caring, self-sacrifice, and unconditional love. These are just some of the ingredients that make marriage different from other relationships. It's also why every civilization since Adam and Eve has had some recognition of this special relationship between men and women that is both unitive and procreative.

Karen and I are blessed with a great marriage. We are best friends, partners, parents, and lovers, but most important, we follow and base our marriage on a vow we made to God. We are far from perfect in any of those relationships, but because our marriage is built on our love of the Lord, the faith and teachings of the Church, and our commitment to do our best to live in the Word, it's made all the difference. We see Jesus as the model for us in marriage as in everything. He gave Himself fully to His Church with sacrificial love never before or since seen. He calls everyone in marriage to give of himself or herself fully to love and serve, just as He has done for us.

As is evident from our story, our marriage, like all marriages, is a work in progress. We fall short daily, but we get up the next day and ask for grace to do our best to love and serve Him through our most important and sacred vocation, our marriage. We realize our marriage is about more than us. Of course, our children are greatly impacted by the state of our marriage, but so is my business, our circle of friends, and in our case, the public. Karen always says, "The most important gift we can give our children is a good marriage." It's also a great gift to the world around us.

We both were blessed by having great role models. Karen's parents were in their sixty-seventh year of marriage before Karen's dad passed away in 2013, and my parents, who didn't marry until they were in their midthirties, made it to fifty-five years before my dad died in 2011. Their relationships were very different; Karen's parents were college sweethearts and lovingly devoted to each other and their marriage, and my parents were a tough, career-driven couple. Our parents were well-educated, hardworking survivors of the Great Depression and World War II, and both couples had a full understanding of marriage and the kind of love that is necessary for its success.

Our marriage is built on the solid foundations of our faith, but tragedy shakes your faith. The death of a loved one can even crack the foundation. Losing a child or having to deal with a child with severe disabilities can topple the entire edifice you have built. It can also destroy a marriage, as we have seen, living in the world of families with disabled children.

Bella's arrival did shake our faith at first. How could it not? We had just finished sixteen years of intensity in the House and Senate, culminating in a humiliating loss by a huge margin. We had just moved into a new home. We were juggling homeschooling the younger kids while shuttling the two older ones to high school. I was trying to discern a new career path, while trying to earn enough money to support the family for the time being. And we had a new baby who could die at any moment and who would require constant care for however long she lived. A new home, new job, new schools, new baby: any one of these presents huge stress. Naturally, we asked, "God, why us?" Why would God take another baby from us? How could the God who loves us unconditionally give us another heavy cross?

When Bella came home from the hospital, we knew her condition required 24/7 care. That was daunting, but I must admit I didn't dwell on it. Karen was so fragile I needed to focus more on loving her and encouraging her. While Karen was caring for Bella and putting all the pieces together at home with the doctors and medical equipment suppliers, I was being Mr. Dad to the rest of our clan. I am by nature an optimist, and particularly so when times are tough. I am also a Martha, not a Mary (see Luke 10:38–42), and I like to express my love through service. So being the rock who held the family together was natural for me.

But what kept me positive had more to do with my faith than my general disposition. After Gabriel died, I dove deep into trying to put his death in a positive perspective. I found the most satisfying advice from Saint Thomas More. More has always been one of my favorite historical figures. In fact,

I hung a portrait of him directly across from my desk when I was in the Senate, so every time I looked up, I saw his picture.

When Henry VIII imprisoned him, More wrote letters to his daughter Margaret, trying to help her understand why he was willing to be executed rather than assent to the king's divorce. He explained that while he fully embraced his career, his family, and his life, his purpose on earth was to keep his eye on God in heaven. He looked at all his earthly duties through the lens of eternal consequences. As he said at his execution, "I die the king's good servant, but God's first."

More was no mystic hermit or cloistered monk; he was a devoted family man, a world-renowned author, an educator, a lawyer, a judge, and at the time of Henry VIII's divorce, Lord Chancellor of England; he was King Henry's right-hand man. The play, then movie, *A Man for All Seasons*, aptly described this Renaissance man as, first and foremost, a follower of Jesus Christ and a devoted man of the Church.

Faith—how much do we really believe what we say we believe? Jesus said, "If you had faith as a grain of mustard seed, you could say to this sycamine tree, 'Be rooted up, and be planted in the sea,' and it would obey you" (Luke 17:6). More had faith and therefore was able to detach himself from many of the earthly restraints that keep us from understanding God's perfect plan for our lives.

One particular letter to his daughter stands out as an illustration of his otherworldly perspective. As his execution approached, his daughter had written him, excoriating those who once served with and were friends of More's, but had since turned against him. He admonished her for her lack of charity toward them with this stunning analysis:

Bear no malice or evil will to any man living. For either the man is good or wicked. If he is good and I hate him, then I am wicked.

If he is wicked, either he will amend and die good and go to God, or live wickedly and die wickedly and go to the devil. And then let me remember that if he be saved, he will not fail (if I am saved too, as I trust to be) to love me very heartily, and I shall then in like manner love him.

And why should I now, then, hate one for this while who shall hereafter love me forevermore, and why should I be now, then, an enemy to him with whom I shall in time be coupled in eternal friendship? And on the other side, if he will continue to be wicked and be damned, then is there such outrageous eternal sorrow before him that I may well think myself a deadly cruel wretch if I would not now rather pity his pain than malign his person.[1]

It is one thing to write such a letter as an academic exercise, but More wrote this letter in the Tower of London as he was awaiting execution. This was faith full-on, and I wanted it. More's admonition had penetrated my soul. Could I, or anyone, in this day and age have the discipline and equanimity to adopt it as a guidepost in dealing with both the slings and arrows of public life as well as the most personal of crosses?

I prayed for the peace and strength that come from true faith, particularly after Gabriel died. I took great comfort in my belief that Gabriel was in heaven, and if I *really* believed it, then I should not simply be in peace but full of joy. I first wondered if it were possible to attach my mind and my heart to this eternal perspective and, at once, detach myself from all the earthly thoughts and emotions.

Looking at More's life, I realized the answer was clearly yes, it was possible, but as I contemplated such a course, I struggled with whether I wanted to walk down that path. Would my family really understand this detachment? In the years after Gabriel's death, I would on occasion journey down that path, but that resulted in many painful moments with Karen. Why wasn't I feeling the constant loss and pain she was feeling? That made me question whether I was really at peace with my faith. Was I simply compartmentalizing and walling off my emotions?

As time passed, we both came to terms with losing Gabriel, but the battle continued to rage in me to claim More's other-worldly faith as my own. I knew it was the only way to truly be at peace with his loss, but particularly in the job I held, it was the only way for me to weather the storms of standing for God's truth in an increasingly dissenting world. For years, people would tell me that I must have a thick skin, when in reality I was holding on with a thinning faith.

When Bella arrived twelve years later, I faced another test of faith. Was I willing, once again, to accept God's perfect will even if it meant losing another child? Could I accept God's will if she survived; could I accept a life dedicated to caring for a fragile child with severe disabilities? And just as important, could I embrace this cross with joy?

Oddly enough, for the first few months of Bella's life, I had been so convinced by all the doctors and literature that she was going to die, I decided to engage in serving my family and pre-paring everyone for the day when Bella would leave us. Losing Gabriel was horrible, but I feared that losing a second child would be twice as devastating to Karen, and particularly to our now much older and more aware children. I had to keep my eyes and heart for Bella fixed on eternity, not on the world. I would treat every day as a joyful gift with no expectation of tomorrow. None of our children is ours; they are all gifts from Him. Our responsibility is to make sure they return to Him on the last day, and with Bella, that was assured. Praise God!

I kept all this to myself, because Karen was in a daily—no, hourly—war to give Bella every possible chance to survive and thrive. As it turned out, we had very different assumptions as to God's will for our little girl. Karen's assumption was that since Bella had survived longer than most T18 children, it was God's will that she would make it.

I wanted Bella to be the miracle Karen believed she would be, and I stood at Karen's side to give Bella every chance to be that miracle. I also looked at the odds, however, and assumed that God's will was to take Bella to Him much sooner than we hoped. I could feel Karen's disappointment anytime she sensed my willingness to accept and embrace God's will for our little girl, whatever it was.

Karen was convinced from the moment we heard the diagnosis that Bella would be different from all the tragic stories we had read and heard about. Her convictions proved to be true. As the days and weeks passed, it became clear it was not God's plan to have Bella quickly pass through our lives. Our mission this time was to learn to embrace the cross of caring for a fragile little one who would never be able to care for herself, to accept her as she is and to love her as we loved all our children, all the while knowing Bella's light is a candle in the wind.

With Gabriel I had to understand and accept God's will,

then try to go on with my life as it was before he was born. With Bella, I again had to understand and accept His will that my daughter was probably not going to live long, but she was still alive. So, I had to both deal with the impending death of a child and at the same time change my life to care for her and an equally fragile family. Unlike our experience with Gabriel, our day-to-day lives had changed, and things would never be the same again.

As we all came to grips with this new reality, I was amazed to witness Karen fully embrace it. I had seen this resolve and quick thinking in Karen before when our other children were in an emergency situation. She drew on all the skills she had developed as an intensive care nurse, together with her wisdom learned from years of experience dealing with crises, to organize and provide incredible care for our children. She realized that Bella would need this type of focus twenty-four hours a day, and that is exactly what we provided. She was convinced God had given us this child because we were best able to provide the care Bella would need to live a long, fulfilling life.

I accepted Karen's perspective and joined her in caring for Bella as best we could, but I had mentally and emotionally prepared myself for the alternative. What I hadn't prepared myself for were the profound lessons to be learned when you embrace the cross of caring for a disabled person. I had always misunderstood the caring for someone who couldn't walk and talk—or even feed or clean or do anything else for him- or herself—as a labor of love. I always admired people who would give themselves in such a selfless way, never expecting or getting anything in return. Like all of us, I had my moments of generosity and even selfless giving when I expected and even wanted nothing in return, but they were only moments, not a lifetime habit.

This life with Bella was an unconditional love that wasn't fleeting; it was constant and often trying and most inconvenient. Karen led the way in our family, but after some eye-opening experiences that I will detail later, I finally joined her in giving myself completely to Bella. Joining Karen was a gift unto itself in our marriage, but so many other blessings also flowed from this unconditional love.

Perhaps the most profound revelation happened on a day Bella was suffering from another respiratory infection. I had just spent an hour or more administering a round of therapies for her and was now standing above her crib, looking at her as she struggled to breathe. She was so fragile, so vulnerable, so totally dependent on us, and none of that would likely change for the rest of her life. Unlike the rest of our children, whom we love just as deeply, Bella will never be able to do anything for us. She will never clean the dishes, make her bed, or make me a cup of soup when I am sick. She is totally disabled, except for, thank God, one thing. She can love.

Bella knows me and lights up like a Christmas tree when she sees me, as well as the others who love and care for her. Standing next to her crib, I became overwhelmed with gratitude that God gave her the ability to know us and clearly express her love for us.

As I thanked God for giving Bella that gift, it suddenly dawned on me that my relationship with Bella is like the Father's relationship with me. Like Bella, in the eyes of the Lord I am totally disabled. And like Bella, all I can really do for Him, all He really wants from me, is to love Him.

This revelation spurred me to think: *Am I as excited to be with our Lord as Bella is to be with me?* Bella is happiest when she is in our arms. *Am I most content when I am close to our Lord?* My relationship with Bella is different from any other. It is as simple as it can get. I love her and she loves me. There are no expectations, no disappointments, no drama, no bad days, and no arguments. Bella is just her same adorable self every day.

I look in her crib in the morning, and she either greets me with a big smile or lets me know she needs a few more minutes to get that smile ready, but it always arrives just in time to steal my heart away. Yes, every day she needs to be bathed, dressed, fed, and sung to. Well, she doesn't have to be sung to, but singing to Bella is a guaranteed way to brighten up your day. She loves it, particularly if you include her name in the words to the song. I have gotten pretty creative with lyrics over the years!

We have exercises to do with her to strengthen her muscles and bones, and I often exercise with Bella, literally. She loves to be lifted in the air, so I lift Bella instead of my weights when I do Bella bicep curls and Bella bench and shoulder presses. Let me assure you: I tire out before she wants to quit!

She loves it when I dance with her and swing her around. Now that she is older and bigger, Daddy can dance longer and roughhouse with her more than Mom can, so it is a special time for the two of us. Bella doesn't like the water, but we take her into the pool every now and then, and that is strictly a Daddy event. It takes a while to ease her in to avoid frightening her, but once we are in, she has a ball.

From time to time we notice little changes; for instance, she will discover a different part of her body or make a slightly different sound. But mostly it's the same. At times it makes me sad that she can't do more, that she can't learn more, but in the end does any of that really matter to our Father in heaven? She is who God made her to be. Bella's relationship to all who know her is one-dimensional and in many ways perfect. She loves unconditionally and is loved the same way.

II

LOVE IS PATIENT

• *Karen Santorum* •

Time is too slow for those who wait,
Too swift for those who fear,
Too long for those who grieve,
Too short for those who rejoice,
But for those who love, time is
Eternity

—HENRY VAN DYKE

S itting at our kitchen table, I watched the spring rain slide
down the windowpane outside. As dusk settled around
us, the house was unusually still. Hearing the drops ping softly
on the sill, I turned to Rick. "Do you believe it's God's will?"

He put his arms on the table and leaned closer, "Do you?"

I looked back outside. This time, I saw a bird dart through the rain from one tree to the next, then back again. My heart went back and forth, torn like that little bird. I couldn't count the number of times we'd had this conversation, prayed through this decision together, and sought advice from wise friends and mentors. As much as I hesitated and fought it, I knew my answer.

But I also knew the fear and apprehension building up inside of me. I would temporarily lose my husband in the service of the nation. Bella's care, and the care of my entire family, would fall predominantly on my shoulders. Our family life, that we had worked so hard to stabilize in the last few years since Bella's birth, would be thrown into chaos. It would be a personal and political crucifixion.

I did not want it. I did not want the burden or stress of being back in the political arena. But I wanted to do what we believed was the will of God. I wanted to love and serve Him, and after much thought and many prayers, we believed this was God's will for our lives. I knew in my heart that Rick should run for president of the United States.

Bella sat next to us in her high chair. She wrapped her hand around my finger, then burst into giggles. I smiled; then Rick and I both started laughing. I think she knew something had to break the intensity of my thoughts! Bella always brings joy, which is a particular blessing in such a moment. Her laughter reminded me of one of the biggest motivations Rick and I had discussed for becoming involved in the presidential race.

We knew that if the Affordable Care Act passed, lives like Bella's would be marginalized and deemed unworthy of "cost-efficient" care. It was the Affordable Care Act that put the fire in me. So, with all these reasons in mind, I knew what we had to do. "Yes, I will love you and support you," I answered, then looked at Rick and smiled. Squeezing his hand, I said, "Let's give it everything we've got."

In June 2011, after months of prayer, conversation, and analysis, we announced that Rick was running for president. Standing on the steps of the Somerset County Courthouse in Pennsylvania, our family surrounded him as we began this journey together. We announced his candidacy in Somerset because that was where Rick's grandfather had come when he emigrated from Italy in 1923. Like many other immigrants, Peter Santorum had come to America with nothing. He witnessed the rise of fascism in Italy and knew he would rather die than live to watch his children march with Mussolini. He wanted a better life for them, one where they would have the freedom to pursue the great "American dream."

Leaving his wife and three children behind, he worked in the coal mines and saved every penny to bring them over. Five years later, their family was reunited in America; Rick's father was seven. His family settled in Johnstown, Pennsylvania, where his grandfather worked in a coal mine until he was seventy-two. Two generations later, his grandson became a United States congressman and then a United States senator who represented the same state his grandfather had come to so many years before. Now, this grandson was announcing his bid to become the next president of the United States. Their story testified to the potential of the American dream. With hard work and determination, a coal miner's grandson could realize improbable dreams.

On that warm spring day on the courthouse steps, Rick explained how his grandfather's sacrifices made it possible for him to be there that day. Rick and I were committed to combating the growing power of government that threatened the realization of the American dream for so many others.

We assembled a team and got to work. But we had a lot to learn. Rick often quoted a line from one of his favorite movies, *Field of Dreams*, changing just one word: "If you build it, *they* will come." And he was right, because as the months unfolded, more and more people arrived from all over the country to volunteer to work for the campaign. They believed as we did; it was the belief in Rick's vision for America that sustained all of us. We worked tirelessly from first thing in the morning until late at night. We had no money and no media coverage. It was an uphill battle against all odds, to say the least. I remember looking at the early national polls from the summer of 2011. They were so discouraging and frustrating that I stopped looking at them.

During the campaign season, a typical day on the home front was filled with a different type of intensity than that of my husband. As a mom, I juggled the demands of family life while also trying to be as active on the campaign trail as I could. With seven kids, ranging from ages three to twenty, Rick and I became creative with our campaign strategies. "Family-focused" became a campaign slogan, but it was also how we operated. We understood the balancing act and just how humorous it often was. Sticky fingers, stained clothes, and frantic searches for a bathroom seemed to precede most of our events.

As his schedule became increasingly demanding, Rick told the kids that he loved them and missed them every day and that he was doing this for them, because he wanted to heal the state of our nation. We discussed the issues with the kids frequently. The older ones were especially engaged, and we sat and listened to their thoughts on everything from war theory justice and medical ethics to immigration, education, and current events. We discussed some issues from a historical perspective, others from a religious and moral perspective.

During the nights Rick was home, we had an assembly line at our kitchen table for our mailings. We saved money and the kids felt involved. Rick signed the letters, one of the kids would fold them, one would stuff them in the envelopes, the unlucky third would lick the envelopes, and the last would stamp them.

As Rick traveled more and more, taking care of Bella became a twenty-four-hour job. Although we had a wonderful night nurse named Erin MacEgan with us during the campaign, her absence was certainly felt the nights she was not there. We often joked that Bella had a college student's sleep schedule. Full of energy, she would stay up and want to play, often until the wee hours of the morning. People often watched a very tired mommy giving interviews!

In the summer of 2011, we packed up our family and moved out to Iowa for a little more than a month so Rick could campaign more easily. Our focus was rallying enough supporters to have a decent showing at the presidential straw poll in Ames. We told the kids this would be our family vacation, our summer "adventure." (Insert a wink and a nod here.) Each of them was truly so sweet, supportive, and eager to campaign.

We packed up our Ford truck, old Suburban, and a Jeep, and hit the road. Our family of nine; Bridget; Erin; my dear sister-in-law Nancy, who is Rick's scheduler; my ten-year-old niece, Olivia; and my nephew Matt somehow fit our lives into a few cars and a precariously filled U-Haul trailer. It was truly a family affair. I'm pretty sure someone made a movie or TV show about this trip. I think it was called *RV* or maybe *The Amazing Race*!

From Pennsylvania to Iowa, it's roughly eight hundred miles. And with Rick as the captain of the caravan, stopping was not an option. But little tummies and little bladders have a way of speaking very loudly. We stopped more frequently after choruses of "I really have to go!" and "Are we there yet?" I waited for Rick to confiscate anything drinkable within their reach, but the kids seemed to do a good job of getting rid of things on their own. The old expression is true that "there's no use in crying over spilt milk." I can also tell you that there's no use in crying over spilt juice or formula.

There are many things I thanked God for on that trip, such as coloring books, magnetized travel board games, books on tape, portable DVD players, and twenty questions. I drove the Suburban carrying Bella, Peter, Patrick, Erin, and Olivia. I loved stealing glances in the rearview mirror. The three little kids had so much fun playing peekaboo with Bella. She'd squeal with excitement when one of them popped his or her hidden head up from the backseat. They'd given Bella one of her stuffed animals and played a lot of games with her. All I could hear from the driver's seat was a lot of laughing and carrying on when they were awake and complete silence when they fell asleep.

Somewhere off Interstate 80, we found the world's largest truck stop. (This is a real place.) In the gift shop, Peter and Patrick were in heaven among the John Deere tractor toys while John and Daniel looked at the different camouflage gear. Elizabeth and Sarah made a beeline for the DVD rack through the dream catchers, beef jerky, and coyote T-shirts. After a hundred episodes of Veggie Tales, they wanted some variety but weren't as excited about the selection there, even after Daniel tried to convince them that a documentary about engine building could be "really cool."

Rick held Bella outside and walked around to stretch his legs and get some fresh air. We still avoided taking her inside crowded places, even when it wasn't cold and flu season. Nancy and I went to Chick-fil-A to order lunch for everyone. "Yes, that's correct," I said to the girl at the cash register. "I did just order six peach milkshakes and eleven chicken nugget meals (with no drinks). To go, please."

Nearly fifteen hours after starting, we crossed into Iowa. By then, the kids had lost track of how many corn and soybean fields we'd passed. As the passing landscape became increasingly flat, they started counting tractors, cows, and tractor trailers. Eventually we pulled off the interstate, and they narrowed their search to simply tallying how many cars passed us in the opposite direction. After driving through many quaint towns and down some dusty dirt roads, we made it to our destination: Oskaloosa, Iowa.

Steve and Jan Boender are some of the most down-to-earth, generous, and kind people I have ever met. When Rick was in Iowa on a previous trip, they had thrown their support behind our campaign after hearing Rick speak. Even though they had never met the rest of our family, they generously offered to let us stay in their converted barn, which provided plenty of space and a cozy home away from home.

One of my favorite memories with the Boenders is one of my first. After pulling up to the barn, we met and talked for a while. As Jan showed me around the barn, I realized Rick, Steve, and the kids had disappeared. I went back outside and still couldn't see them. Laughter came from somewhere to my right, along with a rustling sound. They all filed out of one of the cornfields, each with an ear of sweet corn in hand. Rick ran over and said, "Karen, you've got to taste this! It's delicious!"

Taste what? I looked at the corn. They were eating the corn right from the stalk! Rick laughed at my expression. I took a bite. It was the best corn I'd ever had! I had grown up working in a spacious garden and knew the huge difference in taste between fresh-picked tomatoes, green beans, and zucchini, and their store-bought counterparts. But I had never eaten corn like this! It was so sweet and warmed from the sun you could eat it right from the stalk, no boiling, butter, or salt necessary. Grinning, Steve told us this was a perfect welcome to Iowa.

For Jan Boender's fiftieth birthday, she had jokingly told her husband that she wanted a lake. So Steve had started digging . . . and digging . . . and digging. Finally, after a lot of hard work with his backhoe, front loader, and trucks, he had dug a huge lake! It took him two years to fill it with water, and then he stocked it with fish and built a dock. It was the sweetest birthday gift I have ever heard of and a great act of love. Every morning I sat at the lake doing my spiritual reading and saying my prayers. It was a beautiful and peaceful place.

Unpacking all Bella's equipment and supplies took up the entire evening. Traveling anywhere with Bella takes a tremendous amount of preparation. I pack backup supplies to the backup supplies, just to ensure we are prepared for anything in case of an emergency. At home, I've organized a system of deliveries to meet all Bella's needs. From oxygen to formula to feeding pump equipment, I know who is delivering what supply and when. But, when we decided to come to Iowa, I had to order nearly two months' worth of supplies to bring with us. It was a tall order.

We set up Bella's crib and placed many freshly laundered pink blankets inside it, creating a "Bella world." I didn't think she would feel at home without her pink blankets or her stuffed lamb and baby doll. I placed her vital monitor, feeding pump, BiPAP machine, and video monitor next to her crib. We stacked the formula in the fridge, unpacked her clothes, and stored the rest of her supplies.

As I finished, I left Rick to unpack his things. I walked outside onto the wide pine porch and sat down in one of the rocking chairs. The sun was setting over the lake in front of the house. Cornfields sprawled around me in the distance, and the crickets began to sing their twilight song. I heard splashing and looked at the dock. Peter had pushed Patrick into the water. Uncontrollable laughter ensued. Sarah sat in a chair, bouncing Bella, close enough to the action but far enough away for my comfort. Soon enough, the rest of the kids were in the water. Sarah and Bella stood up and watched happily as the others splashed each other. Then they began to twirl. The girls loved twirling with Bella. Around and around they went. I didn't have to see Bella's face to know how it looked. Breathless. Flushed. Giggling. Arms out like she was flying.

Over the next few weeks, Rick and I traveled across the state, usually with some of the kids in tow. Often the older kids would head to the office in Des Moines to work at the phone bank. Bridget and Erin took charge of Bella's care while we were gone, and knowing she was in their meticulous and compassionate care made my trips possible. During our days at the farm, we went fishing, Jet Skiing on the lake, swimming, and, the kids' favorite, ATVing through paths in the cornfields. It was so much fun!

In the evenings, we joked that we had somehow found our way into *Little House on the Prairie*, and I absolutely loved it! Elizabeth played the piano while the rest of us sang, played board games, or read. In the midst of our intensely busy schedules, the Boenders had given us the gift of sanctuary. We could be a family.

Traveling from the northeastern United States into Iowa opened my eyes to many differences between the East Coast and the Midwest. In the Northeast, most people are overworked, overstressed, and buzz around nonstop like busy bees. And I was guilty. People in Iowa also work hard, but they make time for faith and family. Their slower, midwestern pace allows them to cultivate what's important, and they enjoy life. What happens naturally in the Midwest seems to take so much effort in the Northeast. We sit down for family dinner every evening, but sometimes it's a challenge to just get whoever's home around the table.

There were peaceful family moments during our time at the farm, and there were also many humorous ones. One morning, Peter and Patrick had gone fishing with the Boenders' young grandsons. Grinning proudly, they came back holding several fish by the mouth and asked me to clean them so we could have them for lunch. This was way out of my league, and

Olivia wouldn't get near the fish, even though the boys did their best to get her to kiss them. As I watched the fish flop around, I said we should wait until Dad came home. Then the Boenders' seven-year-old grandson piped up, saying, "Well, I can do it, ma'am." A second grader showed me up, and we ate fried fish for lunch that day.

After several weeks on the farm, we moved into a hotel in Des Moines to be closer to the office as the straw poll approached. Once again, we packed up, unpacked, and set up everything. The process was tedious. In addition to unpacking, Bridget and Erin helped me sanitize all the surfaces in our hotel room, set up an air filter, and clean Bella's supplies. She was a happy camper throughout the process. She became our campaign mascot, our "Energizer Bunny," because when we spent time with her, we felt inspired and ready to work. Bella reminded us of one of the most personal reasons we were in this race: to fight for the lives of children like her, both inside the womb and outside of it. And Bella's smiles, bouncing, and clapping hands always made us laugh.

After many hard months of preparation and work, the straw poll finally arrived. An important event for all the candidates, it evolved into a sort of large, political fairground. A national debate preceded the event, and to my frustration, Rick was put at the end of the stage and given very few questions. They had arranged the seating and questions based on their polls. During the debate I kept looking over at my children and saw the disappointment in their faces that their father had been marginalized. Rick is so good on his feet and a truly excellent debater, so I kept praying that he would be given more chances to have his voice heard as time went on.

Despite the obstacles, Rick made a respectable showing at the straw poll, coming in fourth out of a large swath of candidates.

Suddenly, however, our primary concern became Bella. As our last days in Iowa neared, Bella developed a cold that quickly went into her lungs. She wasn't critically sick, but I wanted to get her out of the hotel, where I couldn't control what she was exposed to through the shared air system. Now that Bella was older, I knew she was stronger, but we needed to get her home. The day after the straw poll, we left Iowa and drove home. Bella took the trip like a champ and was soon happily back in her familiar world.

That fall I came to understand I was sharing my husband with the state of Iowa. He spent a lot of time in New Hampshire and South Carolina. He spent the bulk of his time, though, in the Hawkeye State. The Iowa Caucus was January 3, and our kitchen calendar displayed a countdown of the remaining days. Rick conducted many town hall meetings and spoke candidly and intelligently about the issues. He was genuine and never wrote down a speech because all his words came straight from his mind and heart.

In the modern-day world of politics, where too frequently candidates are over-rehearsed and groomed, Rick's authenticity was refreshing. He also held many meet and greets in barbecue restaurants and Pizza Ranches. These were our favorite types of events. Because these initial events were smaller, we could meet with people and talk with them. Rick and I grew up very simply and loved being with salt-of-the-earth folks who were sincere and genuine.

I did my share of campaigning, but as the mother of seven, including a little girl with disabilities, I could not be out on the campaign trail full time. I held down the home front, making meals; keeping up with the laundry; getting the kids to school, music lessons, and sports; getting them together with their friends; caring for and getting Bella to all her doctor and therapy appointments; and doing everything else that goes into a day in the life of a mother. Life was busy, but our home was running smoothly.

I remember sitting at many of the debates thinking I wished someone would do a day in the life of a presidential candidate's wife who has seven children, including a little girl with disabilities. As any busy mother can relate, just walking out the door to get to an event takes so much preparation and organization. And I'm not talking about just me, but also about the kids' schedules and providing for all their needs in my absence. Sometimes my biggest challenge was trying to go from mommy mode to professional "my husband is running for president" mode! I would throw on a dress, and as I was traveling to my first event, I'd be checking my ears to make sure my earrings were in, that everything was buttoned and tucked, and that no mysterious stains from sticky fingers had made their way onto my clothes. Rick and I remember pressing our clothes in hotel rooms at 2:00 a.m. only to have to turn around and leave at 6:00 a.m.

To get through the rigors of the campaign while keeping the family stable took a lot of patience and love. During the campaign, loving my husband, my family, and my country demanded patience, because we were on a runaway train. The pace and stress of the campaign were overwhelming, and the attacks were malicious. People assume that the hardest part of the campaign is the character assassination, but I tell them I was raised to be tough and can handle the attacks and stress. My greatest cross was having to leave my children, especially Bella.

When I returned from any of my trips, my children's hugs healed me and reminded me what was most important in life, that love is selfless and enduring. I often read this passage and found it a great source of strength: "Love is patient and kind; love is not jealous or boastful; it is not arrogant or rude. Love does not insist on its own way; it is not irritable or resentful; it does not rejoice at wrong, but rejoices in the right. Love bears all things, believes all things, hopes all things, endures all things" (1 Cor. 13:4–7). We could feel Christ's presence. He was there giving us the grace and fortitude for the journey. There was a joyful calm and a selfless, loving attitude in my home that could only have come from heaven.

Another terrible cross for Rick and me was to be away from each other. He had never really traveled much in the course of our marriage. One night, as we were talking on the phone, I told him how much I missed him. Rick got choked up and said, "Honey, you're missing just me, but I miss *eight* of you!" Rick scheduled his trips so he could always get home to recharge his batteries.

We made sure our home was a refuge from the world. The kids did their inside chores so the house would look nice. John and Daniel would mow the grass; Sarah, Peter, and Patrick would weed the flowerbeds; and Elizabeth and I would cook and bake. In the cold months, we loved welcoming Rick home with warm oatmeal or chocolate chip cookies and a fire in the fireplace. As soon as Rick walked through the door, he'd be greeted with an abundance of hugs and kisses.

The campaign demanded a great degree of patience from all of us, but love is patient. Rick's love for his country and our family inspired him to join the race, and he patiently took every day as it came, even though he missed his family. My tests of patience came in many forms, but they predominantly surfaced when I missed my husband at home.

Furthermore, throughout all the stress, the children were patient with their busy parents. They joyfully sacrificed because they believed in their father and this nation. And perhaps most noble of all, Bella smiled through all the chaos, the traveling, and many unbearably tight hugs from one of us who needed comfort. She was patient. She always is.

12

LOVE REQUIRES VULNERABILITY

• *Rick Santorum* •

To love at all is to be vulnerable. Love anything
and your heart will be wrung and possibly broken.
If you want to make sure of keeping it intact you
must give it to no one, not even an animal. Wrap
it carefully round with hobbies and little luxuries;
avoid all entanglements. Lock it up safe in the casket
or coffin of your selfishness. But in that casket, safe,
dark, motionless, airless, it will change. It will not be
broken; it will become unbreakable, impenetrable,
irredeemable. To love is to be vulnerable.

—C. S. LEWIS, THE FOUR LOVES

I t was November 19, 2011, my son John's nineteenth birthday, but I wasn't at a birthday party or even with him
that night. I was in a church in Des Moines, Iowa. It was the
Saturday night before Thanksgiving, and I was at a presidential
debate sponsored by the leading cultural conservative group
in Iowa, the Family Leader. The debate was different from the
other twenty-one in that there were no time limits on answers,
and there was a conservative moderator and a relaxed round-
table atmosphere.

It was the most comfortable debate I had ever attended in
all my time in politics. That should have sent off a red flag as
I was sitting there. Over the course of my career, I have ended
up saying some of the most flippant and, I might add, dumbest
things when a friendly reporter was interviewing me. Any of
you who have been interviewed by a reporter may notice that
reporters couldn't be nicer to you as they ask you questions.
Warning: the nicer they are, the more dangerous they are!

Well, the moderator, Frank Luntz, unlike all the other debate
moderators I have ever experienced, was friendly and engaging
and asked heartfelt, interesting questions that revealed sides
of the candidates I wasn't even aware of. I suspect all the above
was why I answered one particular question with such a personal story—a story about my relationship with Bella. I knew
Karen, my campaign team, and I had long ago made a decision to keep her out of the public eye for a variety of reasons,
but when he asked the question about a specific challenge that
had impacted my life or my faith, all I could think of was my
journey with Bella.

Herman Cain was the first to answer the question. I had
not heard the story of his battle with cancer and the role his

wife had played in it, so I pushed the Bella story back down in my memory to focus on his answer. Next, Rick Perry told his hardscrabble life story. It is a great story, but I had heard it several times, so I started debating in my mind whether I even wanted to answer this question, since there was no requirement to do so. Given the nature of the audience who was in attendance and watching on TV, this was probably the best question of the night for people of faith to gain some insight into both a candidate's faith and his or her character. How could I pass it up?

Both Herman and Rick had received a warm reception from the crowd from their, at times, emotional testimonies. Ron Paul jumped in next with his life story that was more factual than heartfelt, followed by Michelle Bachmann's story of her commitment to Christ, which I had also heard numerous times. During those two answers I decided not to do my personal testimony. I had already covered some of my journey in an earlier answer, and it was what everyone else was doing. Finally, I knew I couldn't do it well in a couple of minutes.

I didn't want to tell my story of Bella, but the only other story that came to mind was the challenge of losing Gabriel. Here again, I had shared that story many times with audiences around the country and in my book *It Takes a Family* and in Karen's book *Letters to Gabriel*. I knew from experience, however, that just because you have told a story hundreds of times, it is very likely that it will be the first time the present audience has heard it.

So I started to get comfortable with the idea of talking about Gabriel. I had told it before, I could do it in a few minutes, it answered the question, and it would give the audience an insight into my faith and our personal life without plowing new ground for the press to dig into. I had decided. I would tell the challenge to our faith that came from losing our son Gabriel.

As Michelle finished her answer, I looked out into the audience at my daughter Elizabeth and thought of Karen. She had been at every debate so far, but tonight she was home. Bella had come down with a cold, and while it was not life threatening, there was no way she was going to leave her bedside. It brought a flood of memories of Bella and her illnesses. It's hard to explain what went through my mind in those few moments as Michelle finished her answer to applause, but a wave came over me.

Everyone else had told stories they had told in some cases dozens of times before, and I was about to do the same thing. I felt called to share something raw and unrehearsed—something real. Even though Gabriel's story is deeply personal and profoundly affected my life, I had traveled the path of telling that story. Even though I relive that experience emotionally every time I tell it, it isn't the same as telling it the first time.

What finally tipped the scales to talk about Bella was vulnerability. As I listened to each one of these stories about how the candidates gave their lives to Christ or personal challenges they had overcome, no one really exposed his or her personal failings or weaknesses. None had answered in the spirit of the question to reveal a part of himself or herself that showed a flaw in faith or character.

After Michelle's applause, Frank Luntz said, "Senator, you don't have to."

I responded, "No, I thought about trying to fulfill your obligation for some confession."

I have viewed the video of this debate more than once, and the shots of me while the others were speaking confirmed my recollection that I was not listening intently, but struggling in my own mind for the right story to tell. That internal struggle came out in the tone of my answer. It was, as I said, confessional.

I began, "I was the author of the Partial-Birth Abortion Ban Act, and I remember being on the floor of the Senate many, many nights, talking about all these children who were disabled—who were the target of partial-birth abortions. These were children who—it was found out late in pregnancy that they had a problem, so their mothers wanted to have a late-term abortion. I would go on for hours and hours talking about the courage of parents who would fight [the doctors] just so their children could be born [alive].

"After I left the United States Senate, Karen and I were blessed with another child. Right before the end of the pregnancy, we found that there might be some problems. So, a long story short, Karen delivered our baby, Isabella Maria, early. They immediately took her to NICU and did some testing. Four days later they told us she had a fatal condition and was going to die. She had a condition called Trisomy 18, which is like Down syndrome; Trisomy 21 is Down syndrome. It was Trisomy 18, which is far worse. They said she's lucky to be alive; there is only a 10 percent survival rate at birth. And of the children who survive, 90 percent die in the first year, most in the first few weeks or months.

"Well, we decided to do everything we could; she was our daughter; we were going to help her. And she did well. She sailed through the NICU and after ten days, we decided there was nothing more they could do for her, so we took her home.

I'll never forget the pediatrician doing the exit interview with us. He kept saying to us, 'You know, you realize that your child is going to die.' I said, 'We have the Internet. Yes, we know all about this disorder.' And he talked about how it would probably be a lung problem. She would probably die because of respiratory failure. And so Karen suggested that we should maybe have a prescription for oxygen if she needed some help. The doctor looked at her and said, 'You have to learn to let go.' I said, 'All we're asking for is oxygen,' and he said the same thing to me. Well, then Momma Bear stood up and [interrupted by applause]. So after we got the prescription for oxygen [laughter], we left and went home.

"We went home on hospice care. Little Bella did amazingly well for the first few months, but then she got a cold. She got sick, and that's a killer for children like this. And it was for her in the sense that she quickly went downhill, and before we knew it, her heart had stopped and she had stopped breathing. Karen was able to do CPR. We got the EMTs; we got her to the emergency room. She did okay. She came back, but then a couple of months later, she had the same thing happen.

"This time I was home holding her when it happened. I'll never forget seeing her fail, not being able to breathe. We had a monitor on her. She stopped breathing, and I put her on the bed, and I tried to do everything I could to try to get her to start breathing again. The next thing I know, Karen comes knocking me out of the way with an Ambu bag and does CPR and Bella comes back again.

"We went to the hospital emergency room. And there she is lying on a table. She's about five months old. And she has her hand out on the emergency room gurney. And I went over and

I reached her—reached out and held her finger. For the five months leading up to this, I had been the rock in the house. I was the guy who held everything together. Karen always asked, 'How can you be so—'

"I said, 'Well, you know, I'm just—this is how I deal with things.' And it was a lie; it was a lie. I decided that the best thing I could do was to treat her differently and not love her (like our other children) because it wouldn't hurt as much if I lost her. I was holding that finger, looking at her and realizing what I'd done. I'd been doing exactly what I had fought against with partial-birth abortion. I had seen her as less of a person because of her disability. And I prayed at that moment: *Please, please let her live. I'll do everything to commit to her, and not just her, but to every child like her . . .*

"And so one of the reasons I'm here tonight is because . . . of 'Obamacare.' We've gotten involved in the world of special needs. Bob and Darla [Vander Plaats, chairman of the Iowa Family Leader] can tell you all about it; I'm sure they know it's a different world. And it's a world that, with socialized medicine, for children like Bella and Bob and Darla's son and others like them who I'm sure are in this room, they will not get the care they need. I will fight to make sure that happens. I will honor them." [Applause.]

I recently watched the video of my answer, and it was clear I was being vulnerable and authentic in telling of my relationship with Bella in her first few months of life. Then it dawned on me that the story itself was a story all about vulnerability. I had held back on giving myself fully to Bella because she was supposed to die. Having gone through that heart-wrenching pain of losing Gabriel, I believed I could minimize the pain if

I just held back and didn't commit fully to a relationship with her. I walled off a part of my heart so it wouldn't be vulnerable, so I wouldn't get hurt.

That night in the emergency room, having almost lost her again and seeing her hanging on to her life by a thread, I realized that treating her differently, loving her less, being less vulnerable would only lead to more pain. I would have missed whatever opportunity and for however long a time to love her completely. I was missing the joy that comes with the completely selfless loving of my gift from God. I would miss the memories of those times and the comfort for the rest of my life in knowing I gave Bella my best.

I am now convinced it would have hurt more and forever haunted me had I not had that second chance to love Bella vulnerably and completely. Like so many lessons in life, what you think is simply a horrible incident in your life turns into one of the great blessings.

As it turned out, blessings abounded from my vulnerability that night. When that debate took place, I was at 3 percent in most of the polls in Iowa, and even lower (if that is possible) in national polls. With the exception of Ron Paul and me, everyone on that stage had been the front-runner for the Republican presidential nomination during 2011. At that time, Newt Gingrich had just become the fifth Republican to take the lead in national polls in the past six months (Romney, Bachmann, Perry, and Cain were the others), and reporters were beginning to ask what some would call unkind questions. "When are you getting out? What's wrong with you? And aren't you embarrassed?"

It would be a stretch to say the only debate of the campaign that was not televised by a national network was the turning point in our campaign, but I have no doubt it had an impact. For the next few weeks, the one question I received more than any other as I traveled Iowa was, "How's Bella?" While the nation couldn't watch the debate, caucus-goers did. I was told more than once that they appreciated our love and fight for Bella and the raw vulnerability I displayed when I spoke about her.

My vulnerability at the debate was not well received by everyone. My dear Karen was hurt, and it broke my heart that I hurt the person I love more than anything in the world. She was upset that I shared my personal struggle, and she thought it was too private to open up to the world about. There are things that stay between a husband and a wife. We've been to the depths of each other's hearts and souls, and this privacy is almost sacred ground in a marriage. I should have explained things better, more thoroughly. What probably upset her more were the words I'd used to describe my feelings toward Bella. In the emotion of the moment, what I'd meant to say was not what came out of my mouth.

What I said was "I decided that the best thing I could do was to treat her differently and not love her as much because it wouldn't hurt as much if I lost her." Telling a story for the first time creates energy and emotional connections with the audience because it is so obviously raw. So raw is good, but it's also new and . . . words don't come out the way you want.

I meant to say "and not love her as much as I love my other children—" but that is not what came out.

It hurt Karen because, as the mother of a Trisomy 18 child, she is all too aware of how so many in the world see them as less, and therefore not deserving of being treated like other children. In her eyes one of the most outspoken pro-life warriors, a well-known Catholic, and a dad of a special-needs girl had confirmed that sentiment to the world. I related to her that we had been tracking social media, and no one in the press or even on the blogs had interpreted my remarks that way, but that didn't matter. After this incident Karen was even more opposed to bringing up Bella in the context of the campaign. I agreed, but that moment of exposing the vulnerability that comes with love had sparked an interest in Bella that was not going to subside.

13

LOVE UNIFIES

• *Karen Santorum* •

*"Have you not read that he who made them from the
beginning made them male and female, and said, 'For
this reason a man shall leave his father and mother
and be joined to his wife, and the two shall become
one'? So they are no longer two but one. What therefore
God has joined together, let not man put asunder."*

—MATTHEW 19:4–6

I, Karen, take you, Rick, to be my husband. I promise to be
true to you in good times and in bad, in sickness and in
health. I will love you and honor you all the days of my life."
Staring into the eyes of the man I loved, I uttered these

words as my own eyes filled with tears. Dressed in white lace and standing at the altar in a majestic Gothic chapel with stained-glass windows reaching up to heaven, I promised him, before God, a lifetime of love and fidelity, to honor and to care for him from this day forward. He promised the same in return. Finishing, I placed a gold ring on his finger. Looking at each other, we smiled. He squeezed my hand. In those blissful moments, my heart nearly burst with joy as I anticipated the prospect of forever with this man. I could not have loved him more.

In those sacred, life-changing moments, you envision a lifetime of shared joy and adventure. Two become one. Your journey together begins. When you say, "I do," it is hard to understand the full breadth of those vows. *I do* promise to love you always and faithfully. *I do* promise to honor you and grow with you. *I do* promise to care for you in sickness and in health. *I do* promise to weather any storm. *Any* and *every* storm.

During the sacredness of that Mass, I thought about the Song of Songs from the Old Testament and the mystery and depth of marital love. The covenant Rick and I were entering into joined us together in a sacred union. When we were dating, we would talk about building a stone castle around our marriage so that nothing would ever come between us. Looking around me, I observed that the chapel in which we were being married was built from limestone, something so strong that it lasts forever and stands the storms of time. The architectural details were impressive and breathtaking. All the woodwork in the chapel was made from oak, one of the strongest woods in the world. I prayed this would also be my marriage: strong, stable, and able to withstand any storm that may come our way; however, at that point in my life, I was convinced this life would be spent in a garden, a bed of roses. Sure, there would be rainstorms and maybe a rumble of thunder, but hurricanes happened to other people.

Back when Rick and I were dating, I worked as a neonatal intensive care nurse while putting myself through law school. I took classes during the day and worked at the hospital at night. I was terribly busy but had the energy of a young woman who felt she had the world at her feet. Everything was new, exciting, and promising. Some of the Pittsburgh law firms were interested in hiring me, and on one of the evenings when they wine and dine you, I realized someone other than the law firm was trying to pick me up.

Rick was an associate at the law firm and one of the lawyers who took me out for dinner that evening. We hit it off instantly. I always said it was love at first laugh, because he had me in stitches all night. He was so handsome, carefree, and funny, not stiff or formal. After dinner we went to a comedy show, and he sang Christmas carols all the way there, even though it was early November.

The joy in the simplicity of watching Rick sing as we were walking through the streets of Pittsburgh was refreshing. When Rick and I met, even though on the surface I was on top of the world, I was going through a horrible phase of life. I was an energetic nurse and determined law student but also a foolish girl making a lot of stupid and sinful decisions. I thought that doing whatever I wanted, whenever I wanted, was freedom and that it would lead to happiness. But instead, it only led to loneliness.

I became a slave to my own desires. My self-seeking will became the rule of my life, I didn't have time for God, and I convinced myself that He wanted nothing to do with me. How could He? After all I had done, surely God could only hold disdain for me. Falling away from the grace of God had put me in the loneliest place in the world.

But then it all changed. I will never forget the moment. I was out to lunch with a dear nurse friend of mine, Gretchen, and she simply said, "Karen, God loves you." It stunned me to hear her say this. Because of my wayward ways and lack of formation in the faith, I didn't think God could possibly love me after all my bad decisions. I thought about Gretchen's words constantly for a few days, torn between disbelief and hope. I wanted her words to be true; I wanted to believe I could be forgiven.

A few days later, after a tremendous amount of thought and soul-searching, I walked into Saint Paul Cathedral, the mother church of the Diocese of Pittsburgh. I gazed up at the gables, spandrels, frescoes, and stained-glass windows depicting the life of Christ; it was breathtakingly beautiful, and I was in awe. But my heart was heavy, and I could not hold back the tears. Intimidated by the holiness of the place, I felt small and unworthy to be there. I was also afraid of the huge step I was about to take, because I thought the priest would yell at me; instead, after hearing my thorough and heart-wrenching confession, he was loving and compassionate.

He quoted 1 John 1:9: "If we confess our sins, he is faithful and just, and will forgive our sins and cleanse us from all unrighteousness." I will never forget him saying, "Welcome home. God is so happy you're here." He told me to not be afraid and to allow myself to be purified by the grace of God and to be free from the slavery of sin.

I sat in church for hours, weeping after that very painful but liberating confession. At one point, a sweet elderly lady tapped me on the shoulder and asked if I was all right. Smiling through the tears, all I could say was, "Yes, I'm going to be all right."

Gretchen's and the priest's words completely changed my life. The fact that God loved *me*, even though I had fallen again and again, comforted me and ignited a fire deep within my soul. Despite all my failings, I was welcomed back into God's embrace, and I knew joy that I had not felt for many years. He loved *me* and was waiting for *me* to come home. Forgiven. Free. A love so huge and unconditional was beyond my comprehension. That was when my spiritual journey began.

To this day I thank God with all my heart for His love and mercy. His mercy is infinite, and there is no sin so great that He will not forgive it. The image of the Father standing on the porch and waiting, longing for His lost prodigal son to return home, will always hold a special place in my heart, because that was me. My dear parents, who had prayed for years for me, rejoiced at my return home. I longed to know Christ. I wanted to love Him with all my heart, all my mind, and all my might. It felt so good to be home.

Years later, my spiritual director told me, "Karen, do you ever think God allowed that time for a reason? It made you the passionate woman you are today. Would Mary Magdalene have received the forgiveness of Christ if she had not sinned? Would King David have been filled with humility if not for his sins? Would Saint Augustine have been a great spiritual leader if it were not for his sinfulness? Often it's the ones who have fallen that teach the greatest lessons in faith." There's no doubt that the dark time in my life fortified the convictions I now have.

When Rick and I met, we both knew we wanted more out of

our lives. After my confession, I believed the void we felt could only be filled with the grace of God. When people ask how we met, I tell them God brought us together. After we began to center our lives around our faith, everything changed. I look back on those dating days with a carefree nostalgia that always brings a smile to my face. We were freed and renewed.

Rick and I went to restaurants all over town, trying out every type of food. We went to sports games and concerts, but also had many coffee dates and simple picnics. We would spend hours talking about everything in the world, and we walked everywhere. We went to church and prayed together. He sent the most beautiful flowers: colorful roses, fragrant gardenias, and soft hydrangeas. We had our favorite haunts, shared dreams, and the same faith. It was perfect. And even when it wasn't, we made it better.

One night, when Rick and I got into a squabble about something I can't even remember, I insisted that he drive me home and refused to talk to him. At home, after my phone rang again and again, it stopped, and I thought he had given up. I cracked open a textbook on my bed and tried to focus. Fine. He didn't have to call. Then I heard a clink at the window, and then another one. I walked over to the window and pulled back the curtain. Rick was standing on the grass below with a handful of pebbles.

Opening the window a crack, I whispered, "Go away!"

He smiled. "Not a chance! I'm just going to sing louder and louder until you come down, Karen!"

I closed the window and crossed my arms. As I turned to walk away, the lyrics of "The Way You Look Tonight" drifted up to me. Turning, I opened the window again and said, "Quiet, you'll wake up the neighbors!" He sang louder and changed the lyrics to "I won't go away until you come down here, just the way you look tonight." By then I was smiling as I grabbed my coat. I couldn't help it. He was just too sweet and lovable.

◆　　◆　　◆

At a local hospital, I worked in a neonatal intensive care unit (NICU), which is a specialized area for preemies and new-borns with serious complications or illnesses. It was a large, level III NICU. After working there for several years, I'd seen almost every type of case. From Siamese twins to babies born with all kinds of birth defects, illnesses, or disease, and babies born so small they could fit in the palm of my hand, we helped many special children get another shot at life. I loved working in the NICU and experienced medicine at its best when physicians and nurses worked together, using all their knowledge and skills to stabilize a child and save a life.

Many of the physicians and nurses poured their lives into taking care of those babies. They were special people, very caring and compassionate. I loved the intensity of the triage unit and having the opportunity to hold the babies in the convalescent rooms. Life in the NICU was demanding—on your feet all day, and always new skills, diagnoses, and treatments to learn. Double shifts were common, as the units were frequently short staffed, but I was happy to work overtime because I loved taking care of the babies. I was deeply moved and inspired by the parents who loved and cared for their infants unconditionally, and it broke my heart when babies were abandoned or had to go through the suffering of detox. To this day, I still think about many of the babies I cared for and wonder what their lives are like now and if they are healthy and happy.

On one of our dates, Rick asked me what it was like to work in the NICU. "It's very rewarding work. We see a lot of complicated cases and help a good number of them. I'm lucky enough to work with the smallest babies, most of them with all sorts of health issues and disabilities. It's been very eye-opening."

Nodding, he asked what cases stood out in my mind. As I sat in that restaurant booth, curly haired, career driven, and so young, I remembered a special case. "I once treated a baby girl with anencephaly. She was born without a brain and lived for two days. Her parents were so kind and, do you know, they didn't leave their baby alone for one minute of her two days of life? They held her, sang to her, and loved her for her entire short life. It's their love that stands out so clearly in my mind. Their unselfish, giving love impressed upon my heart." I started to say something more, then fell silent as I poked at my food, brow furrowed.

"What are you thinking?" Rick asked.

Looking back at him, I said, "I don't think I could ever do that. Losing a child would be the worst thing in the world." After a moment I added, "I just hope that never happens to me."

Eight years later, I remembered that night and my words as I watched a grave being dug for a very small casket. In it was my son Gabriel Michael. Named after two of the great archangels, he now joined them in the heavenly host. Several months into my fourth pregnancy, as mentioned in a previous chapter, Gabriel was born prematurely with serious complications. He lived for two precious hours in our arms, knowing only love.

I remember lying in my bed after the funeral. Curled up in a ball, my eyes dried from countless tears and nights without sleep, I stared at the wall. Watching shadows play from a candle on my nightstand and feeling completely drained and empty, I wanted to remain in the shadows, because I felt I couldn't bear to live in the light. In those dark days, seeing the light at the end of the tunnel became a conscious effort. When you lose a child, it's as though your heart has been wrenched out. You feel nothing, then everything. And it is so hard to hope.

Now, after years of marriage, I was so sure I would never be the same again. How could Rick and I be the same again? I'd heard that the death of a child is the hardest experience for a couple to go through. Now, I had no doubts that was true. By this time, Rick and I had weathered many storms together: campaigns, moves, and the daily grind of balancing professional and family life while going at what seemed like supersonic speed during campaigns. Nothing, however, was worse or more challenging to get through than losing Gabriel. A frightening tempest assailed the castle we had built around our marriage, and the rose garden I'd imagined vanished from memory.

We grieved differently, but we grieved together. Both of us felt the emptiness of loss and the acute sting of sorrow. No parent should have to bury a child. There is something so painfully unnatural about it. Angry with God and confused, I thought about how God had spared Abraham the pain of loss by staying his hand and saving Isaac's life. Why did He not spare Gabriel's life? I struggled. And I grieved.

But time healed us, and we found that there truly was a light at the end of the tunnel. We had our three children. We had our faith. We had each other. Through the dark journey in between, when all seemed hollow and without purpose, Rick and I stood by each other. We confided in each other, held each other, opened up, and prayed together. Those open lines of communication and our shared faith kept us close as tragedy tried to drive us apart. I remembered that sacred vow we had made to each other and to God: "I promise to be true to you, in good times and in bad." Losing Gabriel put these vows to the test and purified us, together, through the flames of grief.

During my pregnancy with Gabriel, I wrote a series of letters to my little son, and these letters later became the book *Letters to Gabriel.* I hoped the story of my grief would help other parents who knew the pain of losing a child. Publishing that book also became a way of healing for Rick and me. Together, we tried to live out our vows to love each other, even when we both were burdened by loss. Our emotions were raw, exposed, and honestly expressed. We learned deep lessons about gut-wrenching honesty in our relationship with each other and, in the process, plumbed even deeper into the mystery that lies at the heart of real love.

◆   ◆   ◆

Bella's diagnosis was particularly crippling. I had buried a child once. God could not allow that to happen again. I was sure I could not bear to lose another child, and for the first year of her life, I lived in fear. I reacted as a protective mother and went into survival mode. But as the years went on, I learned how to be a mother again, how to love and care for my child with different needs. Bella brought great joy to our family, and we adjusted to life with our little girl. But the truth is, I felt terribly isolated and alone.

Three years after her birth, Rick gave his testimony about Bella at the Iowa Thanksgiving Family Forum. He told the audience that he had once felt disconnected from Bella, that he didn't let himself fully love her until she was hospitalized several months after her birth. I was stunned and deeply hurt that he would have shared something so raw and private. Unfortunately, as he said earlier in this book, his words inaccurately expressed what had really gone on in his heart and mind. Rick had made it appear as though he did not love Bella, when in fact he did love her. What he'd failed to do was love her completely because the pain from the loss of Gabriel had left a huge hole in Rick's heart. The thought of losing another child was unbearable to Rick, but this was the crucial point he left out of his answer at the Iowa Thanksgiving Family Forum.

Whereas I had carried the fear and pain of loss and translated it into protective and definite action, Rick had emotionally distanced himself from Bella because of that same fear. If he didn't allow himself to embrace Bella completely, he thought he wouldn't be hurt when we lost her. He insulated his heart, guarding it from letting her in until she was on death's doorstep. I could see why he would be tempted to do this. It's almost instinctual to protect your heart from pain. It's a very normal human response to the overwhelming experience of pain, and losing a child is undoubtedly one of the worst types of pain a parent can endure. I knew, and after experiencing it in the NICU with so many parents, I understood. But it is also instinctual to love and fiercely protect your child.

At first I felt heartbroken that Rick would share his story about Bella in such a public fashion. This was an issue I thought should have been kept within the privacy of our family. I revolted at the thought of his even hinting he had not loved Bella, because it wasn't true. I knew that his faith in God and love for Bella were beyond question. His acceptance and understanding of Bella's diagnosis was a process, as it was for me.

Rick could pray, and as heartbroken as he was, he was at peace with what was happening, but he put up a wall, emotionally separating himself from Bella. The distance allowed him to hold it together, but I was drowning in despair as I fought for Bella's life. Pregnancy, childbirth, and nursing have a way of turning a mother into a grizzly bear.

In the first few years of Bella's life, we weren't living at the *foot* of the cross; rather, we were *on* the cross. Rick and I had spent the last nineteen years of our lives on a spiritual journey together. We went to Mass, prayed as a family every day, went on retreats, studied sacred Scripture, and read books to help us grow in our faith and love of Christ. We loved our Lord deeply. But when it came time for me to completely live my faith, I felt as though I had failed my test of faith! The words of Saint Peter kept going through my mind: "Lord, to whom shall we go? You have the words of eternal life" (John 6:68). There was no place to go except to Christ, but at times it felt as if He were so far away.

We had very different understandings of what following God's will meant. For Rick, it meant abandonment to Divine Providence, no matter the outcome. I agreed. But that didn't mean we shouldn't open our hearts to Bella for as long as she was going to be here. In my heart, I knew God had given us our Bella to love, protect, and to fight for, no matter the challenges or personal sacrifice it would entail.

As with any married couple, Rick and I are of different temperaments, and it was so noticeable during this time. He's the cool-headed, steady Eddie, and I'm the feisty Irish woman. I recall a conversation with my dear friend Muriel, and I was bawling my eyes out. I told her I felt like a bear and my claws never came in. I really did not want to feel this way all the time. I wanted to be at peace, like Rick, but at the time it was like being in a war zone, and it was my child I was fighting for.

In the day-to-day of ordinary life, Rick was an outstanding father to Bella. After her birth he cared for her just as he had for our other babies. He held her, fed her, rocked her, sang to her, and was a doting father. He was just so afraid of losing Bella. His heart ached at the thought, and he carried that dread with him for five months. Then, the moment of truth dawned as he stood at the hospital bedside of his five-month-old daughter as she fought for her life. He saw that, although he had gone through the motions of fatherhood, he had hardened his heart out of fear. He wept.

Ever since that day, Bella has had Rick wrapped around her little finger. He has devoted himself to learning all the intricate details of her care: how to feed her with a nasogastric tube and then a Mini button, how to use the feeding pump and syringes, how to administer medications, how to use the oxygen concentrator and cylinders with the nasal cannulas or mask, how to do nebulizer treatments, and so on. Rick, and the entire family, took a two-day course to get Red Cross certified in infant and adult CPR and emergency medicine. He has always been involved with every aspect of Bella's care, every single day. Even when I felt isolated, he was right at my side, loving me, loving Bella, and holding our family together.

Rick's faith and love provided a pillar of strength for our family and me during those painful times, even when I didn't want to see it. He held me through many tear-filled nights, he told me that we *were* going to get through this together, and he took care of me when the pain from my broken heart was too much to bear. We were both hurting and needed each other more than ever. Rick was constantly with our children and me during this time. When Bella was in the hospital, he brought the children to and from the hospital, took them out for ice cream or lunch, and held them as they cried. I remember many occasions when Rick and I would fall asleep on hospital benches sitting next to each other.

At the beginning, when Rick and I contemplated our futures, we had planned our lives by "the rule," never anticipating the exception. As I said, "I do," I thought I knew perfect happiness; I thought I knew love and that I couldn't love him more, but our love has only deepened and strengthened over time. Therein lies the beauty and the challenge of marriage: you share in both together. What could have torn us apart drew us together, thanks be to God.

Anyone who sets out on a journey, seeking adventure, often does so with the intention of being changed. Traveling, exploring, and discovering are all formative experiences. But there is nothing in life that compares to the thrill, the adventure, of journeying through the peaks and valleys of this life with your soul mate. It changed me, and it changed us together as our hearts were refined in both fire and joy.

When newlywed couples ask me for advice, I always tell them it is good to understand that marriage is never fifty-fifty. Sometimes, whether it's emotionally, physically, or spiritually, one of you will need the encouragement and strength of the other. You will give 90 percent. Sometimes you'll receive that.

Believe and love each other through the imbalances. Don't be afraid to sacrifice for the other, because there's no room for selfishness in marriage. The other piece of advice for married couples comes from Ephesians 4:26: "Do not let the sun go down on your anger." Rick always says, "I'm not going any-where, so let's just work it out." Amen.

Rick and I were blessed to have strong marriages to emu-late. My parents were in their sixty-seventh year of marriage when my dad died, and Rick's parents were in their fifty-fifth year of marriage when his father died. They had very different marriages, but they were strong and built on solid foundations. I can still see my parents in the day to day of their loving and affectionate marriage. They were so in love and would look at each other with that special look only true lovers have. The fire of their love never waned, and they truly enjoyed being together. They always lived a Christlike life, worked hard, laughed with sheer joy, sang the funniest songs, read a lot of books, traveled in retirement to their beach home, and took the time to dance. Theirs was a match made in heaven.

I can still see my parents in our garden on the chilly misty mornings every spring as they taught me and my brothers and sisters how to prepare the soil and plant the seeds. They loved working in the garden together. As the sun warmed the earth, my parents never failed to delight when the seeds sprouted into various fruit and vegetable plants. My parents were brilliant, but they were filled with a childlike wonder and appreciation about the world. We watered and weeded and complained, and my parents would sing songs to keep us working.

Our gardens produced an abundance of fruits and vege-tables, and a typical summer meal was a huge and colorful vegetable platter. We'd be up all hours of the night week after week making jams, sauces, and pies. Our conversations were at times deep and insightful—and sometimes really funny—but there was always something to learn. Throughout the years, our gardens were an important part of my formation.

Being in a large family also meant there were always chores to do. We also took sewing lessons for years and made a lot of our clothes. The daily needs and care of a large family were hard work that required patience and fortitude. There's no doubt that the values my parents instilled in me when I was growing up have given me the faith and inner strength to have the marriage and family life I now have, as well as to endure the journey with Bella for these past seven years.

When I think of our time in the NICU and how five words changed our lives forever, it reaffirms in me the truth that hope in Christ is everything. Truth is, He was preparing me for Bella's birth during my upbringing and in blessing me with my parents and family. Bella's Trisomy 18 diagnosis was a sword that pierced my heart, but it was the solid foundation rooted in faith and family that has made all the difference. Without it I could not have weathered the storm, but with Christ as a guiding light and the strength from my family, anything is possible.

◆　◆　◆

The uncertainties of youth allow their own sort of freedom. Back in the younger phases of my life, the unknown, though sometimes scary, evoked feelings of hope, not fear. Unfortunately, I have seen that as you love more and more, fear is a very human reaction. There is more to lose. *Loss*: a word I didn't really understand until Gabriel. I believe that

God gave us the gift of Bella for many reasons, but one of the most important reasons was to revisit and strengthen my understanding of love through the fear of loss.

Through Bella's life, Rick and I both understood that "there is no fear in love, but perfect love casts out fear" (1 John 4:18). As Rick and I said our marital vows, I thought I could not have possibly loved him more, but now, after knowing him for twenty-six years, I do. I did not think that weathering the storms we've gone through together would bring us closer, but in our journey through life, our love has matured and deepened. Our love for each other and for our Lord has unified us through all the ups and downs. The twists and turns of life have brought us even closer together.

Twenty-six years later we thank God every day for the gift of our love and marriage and know we are blessed to have each other. Twenty-six years later and our journey through life continues.

14

LOVE ENCOURAGES SELFLESSNESS

• *Rick Santorum* •

By this we know love, that he laid down his life for us;
and we ought to lay down our lives for the brethren.

—I JOHN 3:16

W hen I speak about the family, I often recite a litany
of firsts. The family is the first economy, the first
hospital, the first school, and so forth. In a healthy family
environment, the family takes care of the needs of each of
its members. Families are the foundation of society, so when

families are healthy, so is the country. There are many reasons families function well. The most obvious are that they know one another and their wants and needs, and they tend to one another's needs by serving one another out of love. It goes without saying that the more members of the family give of themselves to one another in the home, the happier and healthier the family.

While the family has changed and the web of support varies widely, the family still is the place where almost everyone learns life's most important lessons. I mean every member of the family, not just children. Take, for example, selflessness. My parents taught me the importance of service to others, starting first with our family. All of us had responsibilities beyond taking care of our own stuff that served the family enterprise. While we were also "encouraged," to put it mildly, to serve others by volunteering in the community, we all knew that family came first.

I can remember many times when a friend wanted me to come over to help on a project at his house and the first comment out of my dad's mouth was "Did you finish your chores?" or "Did you ask your mother whether she needs your help on something?" It's not that he didn't want to help the neighbor, but family was first, period.

The best way my parents taught me selflessness was by modeling it in their lives. They each worked forty years serving our nation's injured veterans at several VA hospitals across our country. After work they devoted themselves to giving us a shot at the American dream. They were products of the Great Depression, so they learned to defer gratification and save for the future. And save they did. We lived in World War

II–era public rental housing on the VA post all during my childhood. We drove used cars, and, with two or three exceptions, vacations consisted of visiting relatives and staying at their homes. But they saved money in order to invest in our future by sending us to Catholic grade school and paying for our undergraduate college education.

My dad, who was an immigrant to this country and grew up in poverty during the Depression, lived in a company-owned town. His father was a coal miner who gave his family the greatest gift, coming to America. He ended up working in the deep mines outside of Johnstown, Pennsylvania, until he was seventy-two. He was a Democrat and a union man—he was treasurer of the local mine workers union.

Our family would make the two-hour trip to my grand-parents' home in Tire Hill, Pennsylvania, one weekend every month. We would often complain about leaving our friends or missing weekend activities to hang out at their converted duplex on a busy road. The house sat across a creek from the coal mine. When I was a kid, we didn't think anything of the orange-colored creek water or the raw sewage that floated by as we played on the banks. Nor did we think twice about ignoring our parents' warnings and the signs that said, "Danger: High Voltage" as we played on the electrified train tracks that ran from the mouth of the mine.

We went there, no matter the weather, once a month from second grade until we moved to Chicago my senior year in high school. My dad wanted us to realize that family came first even after you leave the house. He also wanted us to learn where he had come from and our heritage. In the end, he was giving his parents, who by then were in their eighties and not able to travel, the gift of time with their grandchildren, and giving us something even more special.

I never thought it then, but some of my best memories now are of the "boring" times I sat on the porch in the summer with my grandfather, listening to Bob Prince broadcast over my grandfather's transistor radio the Pittsburgh Pirate games, and shoveling coal into the furnace with him on a cold winter day, and taking turns with my grandmother stirring polenta in the old copper pot with a hickory stick. Those times helped me learn where I came from, and that helps me understand who I am.

My grandfather rose from poverty to self-sufficiency, but he never did well enough to have money to help his children go to college. As it turned out, World War II took care of that. My dad turned eighteen in 1941. He ended up serving four years in the Army Air Corps, and Uncle Sam thanked him with the GI Bill. He returned the favor by working his entire career as a mental health professional counseling veterans.

I certainly was blessed with great role models of selfless service to others, but it wasn't until I got married that it really entered my consciousness, and it wasn't until Bella that it all fell in place for me.

Karen and I were married three weeks after I won the Republican primary to run in the Eighteenth Congressional District of Pennsylvania and one week after she graduated from the University of Pittsburgh Law School. Our honeymoon was short, but blissful, and we wished it could have gone on forever. We spent a few nights at my parents' beach condo (They weren't there!); then it was back on the campaign trail.

When I met Karen, she was not a fan of politics. She wasn't

apolitical; it just wasn't her thing. That summer she put off studying for the bar exam and went back to work part-time as a nurse to help us make ends meet. I had taken a leave of absence from my law firm, Kirkpatrick and Lockhart, and we needed every penny. In her free time she would join me on the campaign. She was at my side, knocking on doors, working at the headquarters, attending coffees for me, and encouraging me every step of the way. She was the model of selflessness that summer, and she not only did it well, but with more enthusiasm than me.

The odds of us winning the race for Congress were at least a hundred to one. Back then, members of Congress were generally popular, and incumbents had a 95 percent reelection rate. Our campaign was so off anybody's radar that the night we won, the *Wall Street Journal* called the National Republican Congressional Committee to get information on the person who'd won a huge upset victory in the Eighteenth Congressional District of Pennsylvania (me). Not only didn't they have any information on me; they couldn't even tell the *WSJ* my name! We ended up defeating by a few thousand votes a fourteen-year incumbent who outspent me three to one. It was a political miracle that changed our lives and marriage.

My job now not only put our lives in the public eye but also had me working out of both Washington and Pittsburgh. We were young newlyweds expecting our first child, so when a promised job fell though after my election, Karen decided not to get a job outside of the house. Adjusting to congressional life and getting ready for our baby were enough to keep her busy. We embraced the hustle and bustle of all the travel and events as Congress became the focus of our lives.

During our four years in Congress, Karen delivered

Elizabeth and John, which definitely changed Karen's focus to doing fewer congressional spouse activities in favor of full-time mom activities. Coming from a family of twelve children, it was no surprise she was a natural in the role of mother. For the first three years in Congress, we were a busy young family, but our family was in most respects no different from any other.

That changed in 1994 when I announced my run for the US Senate from Pennsylvania. My Democratic opponent in that race was the Senate sponsor of Hillarycare, the Clinton health reform proposal. With many years of experience as a neonatal intensive care nurse and an attorney with an emphasis on health law, Karen is passionate about improving the quality and choice of our medical care system. She was no fan of Hillarycare and was an articulate and credible voice on the subject. So, of course, everyone on our team wanted her out on the stump. But Karen had just spent the last three years doing everything but public speaking, so she was quite anxious about being able to perform at a high level. Karen knew how important her voice was, so she was willing to step out of her comfort zone to talk about these issues in large public forums.

The reason, of course, Karen had not been on the stump for three years was that she was at home raising our two- and three-year-olds, Elizabeth and John. Fortunately, we had two sets of grandparents and a slew of cousins who lived nearby, and they stepped up to help Karen when she was on the road. And she did indeed make a huge impact by speaking to health professionals and women's groups about our ideas on refining our current system instead of turning it over to government control. I would not have pulled off either of my upset victories if not for Karen jumping in with both feet, doing whatever needed to be done to make it happen.

Karen's involvement was invaluable, but it also raised her profile in the media. To some degree that made her and our family fair game for reporters, but Karen is one tough cookie and can handle anything. She handled the press well and was amazing on the campaign trail. We have learned that the media coverage of someone's family and personal lives is directly related to three factors—the office you hold or in some cases aspire to, how visibly involved your family is, and the level of activity or controversy you generate in office.

In my four years in the House, I think it is safe to say that I generated my share of controversy right off the bat. In my first year, I pulled together a group of freshman Republicans, called the Gang of Seven, to go to the public with special perks that we viewed as institutional corruption. Our efforts led to the closing of the House Bank, where in-the-know Democrat and Republican congressmen enjoyed interest-free loans, and the indictment and conviction of two members of Congress, including the chairman of the powerful Ways and Means Committee.

Let me assure you, when you play the role of cop on the beat, particularly as a brand-new member of the club, you'd better be squeaky clean. The old boys went after me and attempted to dig up anything, including personal things, they could to take me down with them. That was a great lesson for me to learn early in my time in Congress—if you are going to rock someone's boat, expect to have your boat thoroughly inspected. It didn't take me long in Congress to figure out there is nothing I did that someone with enough money or power couldn't find out. In a way that was a gift—to have the knowledge that someone is always watching.

Even with all that controversy and attention directed at me, the media and by and large the public didn't throw my family in the mix. That changed when we ran for the Senate. Senate races have become more national in character in the past twenty years because control of the Senate in such a partisan environment means so much. Also, Karen's prominent role on the campaign trail at the time when Hillary was getting so much attention for her role in the Clinton administration was just too interesting an angle for the media to pass up.

It is easy for a conservative to complain about the news media, and during my career in politics, I have done my share. I thought, however, the overall coverage of Karen and her role was fair. It wasn't until I became involved in some particularly controversial issues that it began to change. I found it was one thing to hold yourself out as a conservative reformer, shaking up Congress by unearthing scandal or taking the lead on the Balanced Budget Amendment, welfare reform, health care reform, and even Social Security reform; it is quite another to take the lead on moral and cultural issues. For the first five years in office, I never talked about any of those moral issues because of the political land mines that surround them. They are emotional and potentially divisive, so I steered clear.

When that changed two years into my first term in the Senate, I soon realized the stakes I had raised. It's one thing to be a conservative, but the progressives and the media will not tolerate anyone who has the temerity to vocally counter their views on marriage or challenge their culture of death. Any conservative who is committed to fighting for life from

LOVE ENCOURAGES SELFLESSNESS

conception to natural death and for the freedom to practice your faith, not just in the church but everywhere else, should expect hostility. I always joke that when I started to take on these issues, my children who read the papers thought I had changed my first name to "Ultra." Now, according to the press, I was the *ultra*conservative senator from Pennsylvania.

Something else changes for those of us who are vocal advocates of a moral and decent culture. Your past and every action you take get viewed through the lens of that morality. If you set a high moral standard, expect to be held to it. On the other hand, since your opponents on these issues are not taking moral stands, they are held to no additional standard. In fact, they are often given a pass by the media for any moral indiscretions, while those who take moral positions and fall are called hypocrites.

I want to make a point here about hypocrisy. Of all the criticisms that are leveled, being called a hypocrite may be the most stinging and damaging. It is one thing to make a mistake; it is quite another to have your sincerity, your motivation, and your overall character assaulted by being called a hypocrite. The news media relishes the opportunity to throw around that term to describe a public figure, always a conservative, who has a moral failing that contradicts his or her stated positions.

Take, for example, two married members of Congress, one an evangelical conservative, one a secular liberal, who both have affairs or are both arrested for buying illegal drugs. Which is the bigger story? In the eyes of the media and maybe now even the public, the conservative, of course. Why? The liberal never talks about the importance of marriage and is for legalizing drugs, so in the eyes of the media, there is less moral culpability for his or her crimes. But the conservative is a great advocate for marriage and the family and talks often about the scourge of drugs and its harmful effects on our country, so his or her transgressions are not only more serious, but they qualify as hypocrisy.

The fact is, the conservative could very well be a hypocrite, particularly if he or she was condemning others at the same time he or she was doing the same thing. Also, if the conservative didn't actually believe in the positions he or she publicly stated, then the conservative is indeed a hypocrite. You can sincerely hold positions about what is true and right, however, and try to uphold them in your personal life and, despite your best intentions, fail. Your failure to live up to what you believe is right does not make you a hypocrite; it makes you human.

Why did I need to make the point about hypocrisy? I have seen many conservatives, famous and not famous, who run away from talking about moral issues and have even softened their stances because of the fear of being viewed as a hypocrite.

Karen and I were trying to make our family life as good as it could be. We knew putting God first in our marriage and family would be at the heart of that success. Funny thing happens when you focus on the life of Jesus. You see how He changed the world through the complete giving of Himself. He calls on us to do the same.

In basing our marriage and family life on His example, we committed to put each other and the family before our own desires. That played itself out differently for me than for Karen. Both of us are high-energy, focused people who fully engage in the task before us, so we decided to put in place rules and procedures that ensured our family and our marriage were the priorities we wanted them to be.

The most important rules governed my time. When I was working in DC, I didn't go out for dinner, other than required political events. I made no appointments after 6:00 p.m., so if the Senate, which chronically works into the evening hours Monday through Thursday, finished early, I could go straight home. I worked only one Friday night and Saturday a month, and never on Sundays. When I had to travel, I did my best to get home the same day, no matter what time. If I had an overnight, it was no more than one night. Therefore, I almost never traveled abroad. The very few times I did, they were trips where Karen could come with me.

We have other rules that protect my family and me. I never travel alone with another woman. If there is a woman in a car or plane with me, then we are accompanied by a male volunteer or staffer. That goes in my office too. If I needed to meet privately with a woman in my office, the door to my executive assistant's office would always be open. Although she couldn't hear what was being discussed, she had a clear view of the meeting. We did this not just to protect me, but to protect everyone involved from any malicious behavior or accusations.

I have been very public about my marriage and family being the most important gifts I have, and even at work that commitment is on the top of my mind in everything I do.

As a result, we are often asked to speak about our marriage. About ten years ago, we were doing just that in Wichita, Kansas, at a Catholic conference. Our talk focused on the importance of selflessness in marriage. At a book signing after the speech, an enthusiastic young man named Michael Manhardt came up to us, waving some wristbands in the air and shouting, "This is the answer!"

I asked him, "What is the question?"

He handed Karen and me wristbands that read "F.A.M.I.L.Y." He said, "Have you ever seen the wristbands W.W.J.D.? This is the answer, 'Forget About Me I Love You.'"

As I type this on my laptop, that wristband is still wrapped around my left wrist. Over the years, I have told this story and given away my wristband dozens of times, because that is how Karen and I see our responsibilities inside the family.

Before you start pointing out the decisions I have revealed in this book that are not consistent with this creed, let me say you are right, in part. First, I no more perfectly model FAMILY than I do the moral and ethical teachings of my faith. Like everyone else, I fall short and I confess that to myself, to my family, and to my Savior. As Christians, we are blessed with Jesus' example of selfless love to the point of dying on the cross for us, and with that His gift of forgiveness for any thought, word, deed, or omission that violates His teachings. I always tell my children the important thing is to sincerely try to give yourself to your spouse and family, and then every day honestly assess how you did that day.

It seems almost axiomatic that if you truly love some-one, you would be willing to sacrifice greatly on that person's behalf. We have visions of movie heroes who leap in front of a lover to take a bullet or dive into a raging stream to rescue a drowning child. Those are indeed selfless acts love inspires and are rightly celebrated as heroic.

True, lasting, loving relationships, however, are not built

or sustained on dramatic or spectacular acts of selfless love. I had the opportunity to meet Saint Teresa of Calcutta a few months before she died. She had a wonderful saying: "God does not call on you to do great things; He calls on you to do little things with great love." As I write this in the wee hours of the morning, I am sitting next to Bella as she sleeps, massaging her every few minutes to encourage her to breathe. She has a cold and her nose is stuffed to the point where she can't breathe through it. Because Bella is who she is, she doesn't always figure out to switch to her mouth to breathe if her nose isn't working. That is why I am up and blessed with a few quiet moments to write this chapter of her book.

Tonight is my "little thing" that I do willingly and, in spite of the fatigue, joyfully. Karen was blessed to be on duty all last night when I was away in Columbus, Ohio. If you are a parent, I am sure you could tell your own stories of being up late with a sick child. We had our share with our other children, but being the parent of a severely challenged child is different. It's not the occasional illness or accident; it's every day. Karen and I learned a lot about selflessness in our marriage, but Bella required us to go to the next level.

I was recently with the great writer and motivational speaker John Maxwell at his alma mater, Ohio Christian University. He gave a talk on the qualities of a good leader that summed up what Bella has taught us about the key to selfless love. He said the biggest key is consistency. Before we had Bella I never would have said that in a million years.

15

LOVE BEGETS PEACE

• Karen Santorum •

We draw people to Christ not by loudly discrediting
what they believe, by telling them how wrong
they are and how right we are, but by showing
them a light that is so lovely that they want
with all their hearts to know the source of it.

—MADELEINE L'ENGLE

S tretching out her hand, Bella touched the side of Rick's face as she often does. Her eyes grew wide as she felt his scruff. Pulling her hand back, she released high-pitched squeals of joy and giggling laughter. Daddy was home. Bella greeted him with an animated reception, as she always does. As he tossed her in the air, she threw her head back, smiling and stretching out her arms. Flying. He held her, smiling and talking elatedly. She responded to his tone by clapping her hands and nodding vigorously, so happy that her daddy was home.

We gathered as a family and curled up around the fire, one of the last of the season. Rick had just won the Mississippi and Alabama primaries, putting the tally of states he had won at ten. I was so proud of him and of all his hard work. Elizabeth had been campaigning in Hawaii for ten days, a job she had gladly accepted. Rick and I had just returned from traveling to Puerto Rico with John, Daniel, Sarah, Peter, and Patrick for that primary contest. Finally, all of us were at home, if only for a night. I could not remember the last time that had happened.

Watching the children pass Bella around the room, I reflected on how, in the midst of the hurricane that was the presidential campaign, God had put us in the eye of the storm, where there was peace. There was happiness and serenity in the daily rhythm of our family life that could only have been divine intervention. Each of the children wanted to hold Bella next. She loved the attention and her eyes shone as she joyfully responded to their love. Bella's light soothed our hearts and gave us peace. She had quickly become the anchor for our home life, a joyful and constant presence who would offer only love.

Rick was completely immersed in the presidential race and was extremely busy handling a million demands. As a wife and mother, I tried to balance keeping life at home as normal as possible while having to travel around the country with Rick to campaign. We may have been immersed in a presidential race, but our children still needed to be educated, participate in sports, get to their music lessons, and see their friends. It was a lot of juggling, and I was thankful that while Elizabeth and John were busy working on the campaign trail, Daniel could drive himself and Sarah to school each day.

People always want to know what the hardest part of the campaign was, and I always tell them that I can handle everything except having to leave my children. I've never been good at leaving my kids, and neither has Rick.

Life with Bella made my trips a little more complicated. If I left, Bella needed a nurse with her overnight should any problems arise. Bella's sleep patterns were often irregular, so it was critical to have someone who knew her and her care, should she stay up to all odd hours of the night. I thanked God many times for the blessing of our talented and compassionate registered nurse, Erin MacEgan. Truly a godsend during the campaign, she and Bridget made my campaign travel possible. Bella loves them and always became excited when she saw them. She'd smile, kick, and wave her arms in the air. We called it the Bella dance.

Life at home was hardly normal. After the Michigan primary, the Secret Service had taken responsibility for Rick's security. At home, a Secret Service van was stationed in the driveway and agents patrolled the yard. We were so grateful for their protection. Our detail was composed of honorable, professional, and sharp men and women. We were blessed with good people on our security teams throughout the campaign; our first security detail leader, Andy Patrick, became a dear friend. Knowing that Rick and my family were safe put my mind at ease.

When Rick and I would go to events with six of our children, there was not enough room in the Secret Service SUV, so we had to take our truck. There were a few times when we drove in the lineup with a police car, three Secret Service SUVs, and then our truck sandwiched in between. They drove fast and tight, and our son John drove the truck in the lineup. For John, Daniel, and their friends, it was a teenager's dream come true to drive at eighty miles per hour and not have to worry about getting a ticket! For me, even though John is a great driver, those long, fast trips were stressful at the time, and something we laugh about now.

In April 2012, after fifteen competitive primary contests in which Rick won eleven states and almost four million votes, and after almost a year of intense campaigning, the promises of Easter and a few days off from the trail were enticing. We felt like weary travelers who needed a respite from the journey. Rick came home on Holy Thursday, eager for some time to sleep, regroup, and spend time with the family. Sadly, in the wee hours of the morning, Bella, who had been struggling with a runny nose, got really sick and went into her death spiral.

Her lungs were congested, and she was not breathing enough to keep her oxygen levels up. She was having one apnea after another; in addition, she had a high fever and was tachycardic. When Bella is sick, we immediately call the pulmonologist and start the nebulizers, suctioning, chest PT, various medications, and oxygen if needed. It's a frightening and stressful time. Rick has always been a rock for me during times when Bella is sick. It's extremely emotional for us both, and I must admit that I cry a lot when she's sick. I don't cry while I'm focused on Bella's care; rather, it's in the quiet of the night after we've stabilized Bella that tears come spilling out.

Rick and I had been up with Bella all night, and instead of improving, she continued to decline. Her fever was raging, despite the acetaminophen, ibuprofen, and sponge baths. We were giving Bella frequent nebulizers, but her congestion only got worse. Her oxygen requirements kept going up as her oxygen saturation levels dropped, and her heart rate was frighteningly high. Whatever was making her sick was a nasty bug, and we could not get it under control. We had spoken with the pulmonologist several times throughout the night. In the morning the pulmonologist recommended some treatments, but when Bella did not respond to them, her doctor said we needed to bring her into the hospital.

The last place we ever want to take Bella is the hospital. We're always concerned we'll bring her in for one illness, but she'll catch something else. With the superbugs that are in the hospitals today, and the fact that during cold and flu season the isolation rooms are in high demand, this is a legitimate concern. Because of these concerns, the decision to take Bella to the hospital is one that we always leave up to her physicians, but they also know we try to get through Bella's crises at home. Rick and I, together with the pulmonologist, do everything we can to avoid the hospital, so when her doctor said we needed to bring Bella in, our hearts sank.

Rick radioed the Secret Service agents who were outside our home. He told them we had to take Bella to the hospital. As always, the cars were ready and waiting in the driveway. Since we had the oxygen, monitor, and medications, the pulmonologist suggested we just get in the car and get to the hospital. We could be there by the time an ambulance arrived at our home; in addition, the ambulance would only have been allowed to take Bella to the local hospital and not to the one that had the pediatric unit where our pulmonologist worked.

We bundled up Bella, got into the SUV with her oxygen tank and monitor, and drove to the hospital. At a moment like that, I was grateful that the intimidating, black caravan of SUVs commanded the respect and interest of other drivers as they cleared the way on the road. We made it to the hospital in record time.

Since we did not have time to go all the way to CHOP, we had to go to our local hospital, Fairfax Hospital, which has an excellent pediatric intensive care unit. I must admit that once you're used to the excellence of CHOP, it's really hard going to another hospital, and there is an additional layer of stress added since we were not going to the hospital that we knew and completely trusted. I was nervous going to a place where I did not know the physicians or the facility; however, this was not the same hospital that Bella was in when she was six months old. We will never go back there.

It was a great comfort to Rick and me that, when we arrived, Bella's pulmonologist met us in her room and cared for her the entire time she was in the hospital. Dr. James Clayton, Dr. Sunil Kapoor, and the nurses at Fairfax Hospital took great care of Bella. They were able to get her stabilized, and it was a huge relief when Bella turned the corner. Dr. Clayton and Dr. Kapoor and their team were bright, professional, compassionate, and thorough in their assessments of Bella, and included Rick and me in the decisions regarding her care.

It was no coincidence that Bella was admitted into the

hospital on Good Friday, a day that is highly significant to us as Christians. From the moment our Savior was born, His entire life was directed to the supreme moment when He was crucified and died on the cross. As Bella lay in her hospital bed that day, I thought about Christ's passion and how Mary, His dear mother, must have felt watching Him being mocked and treated with such horrific cruelty.

Anytime Bella was in the hospital, it was like a constant spiritual retreat. I would hold her and stroke her head and pray constantly. My Bible and spiritual books were always with me, and the inspiration from them helped me stay focused on Christ and the meaning of suffering. His cross is the tree of life that gives us our salvation. His cross is the stairway to heaven and God's glory. "If any man would come after me, let him deny himself and take up his cross and follow me," He said (Matt. 16:24).

There were times when I felt as though I were on the cross—not at the foot of the cross, but on it. It was during those moments, when the worries and burdens were crushing me and pulling me down into a dark valley, that our dear Lord filled me with His grace and gave me the strength to see the light through the darkness. My entire being is filled with thanksgiving, and it is a great consolation to know that no matter what happens in life, our Savior will hold us, strengthen us, and walk my family out of the darkness and into the light.

Through Bella's life, I have witnessed one of the most important lessons of Christianity firsthand. When there is no purpose to pain or sickness, it becomes suffering, but when we unite ourselves with Christ and trust completely in His divine providence, we are filled with hope. It is the hope of an intimate relationship with Jesus Christ and that we are one step closer on our journey toward heaven, and heaven is all that matters in life. I don't understand this mystery of suffering; I can only trust that somehow it will all work for the glory of God.

It was on Good Friday that Rick and I, in the midst of caring for Bella in the pediatric intensive care unit, began sifting through the decision to continue with the presidential race or to bow out gracefully. We were immersed in our Lord's passion in a way like never before. Our marriage and children had always been our most important priorities, and having Bella in the hospital tipped the scales of emotion and sapped us of our strength. We had been on a high-speed train and by the grace of God were able to handle it; that is, until Bella got sick. The most important focus for Rick and me was getting Bella better and tending to the hearts of our six other children, who were worried about their little sister.

We gathered the children together in Bella's room, and we hugged and prayed. We listened to their thoughts and wiped their tears. For the entire Easter weekend, we prayed for Bella's health and about the decision to leave the race or continue. By Easter Sunday, that most glorious day of Christ's resurrection and the promise of new life, the decision was made clear in our hearts and minds as we prayed.

Praise God, Bella was well enough to come home the following day. We came home to a house full of pink roses. I have often mentioned that Bella loves pink roses. Initially, the children bought them to congratulate me when we found out we were expecting a girl. They thought pink roses would be perfect for a baby girl, and with time they had become "Bella's flower." We frequently buy pink roses simply because they are cheerful and brighten up the house. Only later did we learn that pink roses symbolize gratitude. Throughout her life, we have had vases of pink roses in the house, an unknown and silent declaration of gratitude. We will be forever grateful for Bella's life, her joy, her impact on our family, friends, and church community. On this particular day, we were especially grateful for her healing.

The Monday after Easter was Elizabeth's birthday, and she was a champion on the campaign trail. She handled everything with intelligence, grace, and strength. We made her birthday a beautiful celebration of her life, and we were all happy that our sweet Bella was home. The following morning we held a press conference, and Rick announced, with me, Elizabeth, John, Daniel, Sarah Maria, Peter, and Patrick at his side, that he was ending his run for president. It was a bittersweet day. Bella was on the path of recovery, but I knew in my heart what the outcome of the presidential race would ultimately be, and I feared for the future of our nation. We had just given the United States presidential race to someone who would not talk about the most important issue and our ticket to success: the Affordable Care Act.

When the presidential race ended, and all the good-byes were said and all the numerous details to wrap things up were completed, Rick and I took a three-week vacation with our children and my dear mom to our favorite place in South Carolina. It was a perfect three weeks, and everyone, including Bella, had the time of their lives! We were finally able to gather around the table as a family for all our meals; we rode bikes for hours on the trails and on the beach; we played board games and laughed the entire time; we soaked up the sun for hours while listening to the soothing sounds of the ocean as we built sand castles and jumped the waves; and we went to church and thanked God for all His blessings for which we were eternally grateful. It was a healing time for our family, and a time when we added a lot of memories that we will always treasure.

It is in our brokenness that we are healed and brought to new life. We are the clay and Christ is the Potter, and it is He who renews our souls.

Elizabeth recently read a passage to me from one of our daily meditations that touched me. It is about a very special boy named Armando. His story reminds us that only through our brokenness do we really grow.

Armando [is] an amazing eight-year-old boy . . .

Armando cannot walk or talk and is very small for his age. He came to us from an orphanage where he had been abandoned. He no longer wanted to eat because he no longer wanted to live cast off from his mother. He was desperately thin and was dying of lack of food. After a while in our community where he found people who held him, loved him, and wanted him to live, he gradually began to eat again and to develop in a remarkable way. He still cannot walk or talk or eat by himself, his body is twisted and broken, and he has a severe mental disability, but when you pick him up, his eyes and his whole body quiver with joy and excitement and say: "I love you." He has a deep therapeutic influence on people . . .

What [many people] do not always know is that they have a well deep inside of them. If that well is tapped, springs of life and of tenderness flow forth. It has to be revealed to each person that these waters are there and that they can rise up from each one of us and flow over people, giving them life and a new hope.

That is the power of Armando. In some mysterious way, in all his brokenness, he reveals to us our own brokenness, our difficulties in loving, our barriers and hardness of heart. If he is so broken and so hurt and yet is still such a source of life, then I, too, am allowed to look at my own brokenness and to trust that I, too, can give life to others. I do not have to pretend that I am better than others and that I have to win in all the competitions. It's okay to be myself, just as I am, in my uniqueness. That, of course, is a very healing and liberating experience. I am allowed to be myself, with all my psychological and physical wounds, with all my limitations but with all my gifts too. And I can trust that I am loved just as I am, and that I, too, can love and grow.[1]

> *Non nobis, non nobis, Domine*
> *Sed nomini tuo da gloriam.*
>
> *Not to us, not to us, O Lord,*
> *But to thy name give glory.*

16

LOVE CHOOSES JOY

• *Karen Santorum* •

We have to choose joy and keep choosing it.

—HENRI J. M. NOUWEN

D ay 2,553: Wednesday is an important day in the Santorum house. On May 13, 2015, Bella turns seven. As some people can imagine, having seven kids in our family, we do a lot of birthday parties. Various decorations, party hats, and reused gift bags are always floating around the house, waiting to be used in the next celebration. Our house is a happy one, full of life. That being said, Bella's birthday is always uniquely joyful and the cause of grateful reflection.

Sitting on the lawn in front of our house, I watched as Bella sat alert in her stroller and played with her toys, kicking her dangling, sandal-clad feet back and forth. She looked up at me every now and then to smile or talk. She doesn't talk like any other little girl. She has her own language; as previously mentioned, instead of speaking English, we say she speaks "Bellish."

The birds' songs occasionally broke her concentrated focus on her baby doll. I couldn't help but laugh as Sarah enthusiastically piled dandelions on Bella's lap, showing her how to blow the "white fairies" into the wind. "Make a wish, Belle," Sarah whispered. *Make a wish*, I thought. *A birthday wish for many more years to continue rewriting the medical textbooks, proving the statistics wrong, and offering hope to other families with Trisomy 18 children.*

I watched Bella's dainty fingers grab the stems, spraying the fairies. Her smile broadened, sea-blue eyes watching the fairies soar up and into the wind. Make a wish. I have made wishes and prayers for you, little one, more than I know how to count.

When Bella was hospitalized, we prayed constantly and found strength in sacred Scripture:

> *When the cares of my heart are many,*
> *thy consolations cheer my soul.*
> (Ps. 94:19)

I prayed for His consolations, to be comforted by my Father. As I sat there with Bella, I couldn't help but smile at how He had answered my prayers. Bella's condition and sicknesses have given my heart anxiety, but her joy and her life have been my consolation. When she was born, He led me down a path of growth that was ultimately drawing me back toward Him. When I looked back on the past seven years, I saw that the source of the journey so often riddled with anxiety and suffering was the same source of my consolation: this smiling little girl.

Bella's life is founded on the prayer, the wish, and the hope that my family will be graced with one more day with her. Nearly seven years later, the outward effects of her condition are hardly apparent physically. Even though, in our minds, she will always be our baby, she falls in the typical height range for a child her age, and her condition has no physical manifestations, save her sweet little fingers that she likes to hold in the typical Trisomy 18 fashion.

Each day is marked by small but invaluable moments. I've watched her stare into Sarah's eyes as she sings her songs or be in stitches as Daniel makes goofy voices. I've laughed as she dances with John to the Beatles or giggles as Patrick bounces her on his lap. I smile whenever Bella plays the piano with Lizzie, hands on top of her big sister's. I've witnessed her drive as she walks with Peter, so proud of herself when we sing the "Bella song" in praise. The song is a new take on an old tune, but we are quite sure Bella thinks it was written just for her, because she never fails to light up when we sing it:

> *We love you, Bella*
> *Oh, yes we do*
> *We love you, Bella*
> *And this is true*
> *We love you, Bella, we do*
> *Oh, Bella, we love you!*

Simple joys. In those moments, life is sweet and we are grateful. For each rough day, there are a hundred healthy days in the sun. Ironically, the bad days make the good ones even better. They provide perspective, which in turn changes our attitudes. We appreciate the days of health and happiness all the more because we know they are precious gifts.

Initially, life with Bella was a crash course on learning to see the joy of the moment. When the present is all you are sure of, you can either live in fear of the future and be consumed with the predicted pain, or you can choose joy, making every blessed moment one of beauty. When Pope Benedict XVI arrived in Portugal on May 12, 2010, he discussed one of his favorite themes: beauty. He told the pilgrims who had gathered:

> Dear friends, the Church considers that her most important mission in today's culture is to keep alive the search for truth, and consequently for God; to bring people to look beyond penultimate realities and to seek those that are ultimate. I invite you to deepen your knowledge of God as He has revealed himself in Jesus Christ for our complete fulfillment. Produce beautiful things, but above all make your lives places of beauty.[1]

"Make your lives a place of beauty." When I read those words, I immediately thought of our little Bella. Bella makes the Santorum house a place of beauty, and she doesn't need to change to do that. She doesn't need to have one less eighteenth chromosome. God created her, and He calls her "beloved." He knit her together in my womb, has numbered the hairs on her head, and knows her innermost being. *She is beautifully and wonderfully made!* She has impacted the lives of many, helping them to find the way of beauty and to choose joy, no matter what the prognosis.

In Plato's *Republic*, Socrates crafted a famous story about men who are chained in a cave. Staring at blank walls, they see only the shadows that are cast from the fire behind them. Unable to reach beyond their limited experience, they accept these shadows as reality and never know what is beyond these wisps of truth. They cannot break their chains or crawl out of the cave and into the light. Socrates said that a philosopher, a lover of wisdom who sees the truth and leads others to it, must save them.

To many, Bella is the one in the cave, but I know that it's quite the opposite. I am the one staring at the walls. We all are. In *The Weight of Glory*, C. S. Lewis explained this paradox of the human condition, saying, "We are half-hearted creatures, fooling about with drink and sex and ambition when infinite joy is offered us, like an ignorant child who wants to go on making mud pies in a slum because he cannot imagine what is meant by the offer of a holiday at the sea. We are far too easily pleased."

In their beauty, wisdom and truth are capable of changing minds. Yet, there is a different type of beauty that leads man out of the cave of his own primitiveness: the beauty of love. Love in its purest form is completely selfless, strong in its gentleness, and the virtue that gives value to all action. "If I have prophetic powers, and understand all mysteries and all knowledge, and if I have all faith, so as to remove mountains, but have not *love*, I am nothing" (1 Cor. 13:2, emphasis added).

Love is the greatest of all virtues, the necessary intention behind all sincere and good actions, and it happens to be the quality our Bella practices best. She gives love. Through her constant, radiant love, she leads. In the midst of the most mundane days, her smiles and sweetness draw us up and out of the caves of our own mediocrity, reminding us to rise and live joyfully.

On my own journey of faith, Bella's silent witness to the power of love has transformed me. Perhaps this new perspective is best summed up in a passage by G. K. Chesterton, who said, "Let your religion be less of a theory and more of a love affair." Bella has a simple heart, one that will never understand the intricacies of theology, but she practices the core of the Christian faith: love.

As I watched Bella and Sarah play on the lawn that spring day, I was reminded of how Bella's love continued to restore an appreciation for the simple joys of life, like dandelions drifting in the wind. She will always be innocent, always childlike. It was our Lord who said, "Truly I say to you, unless you turn and become like children, you will never enter the kingdom of heaven. Whoever humbles himself like this child, he is the greatest in the kingdom of heaven" (Matt. 18:3–4).

In a world too often focused on instant gratification and personal satisfaction, it is no wonder that lives like Bella's are considered "inconvenient." Joe Klein talked about just that in an article he wrote for *Time* during the presidential campaign:

I am haunted by the smiling photos I've seen of Isabella with her father and mother, brothers and sisters. No doubt she struggles through many of her days—she nearly died a few weeks ago—but she has also been granted three years of unconditional love and the ability to smile and bring joy. Her tenuous survival has given her family a deeper sense of how precious even the frailest of lives are. . . . I also worry that we've become too averse to personal inconvenience as a society—that we're less rigorous parents than we should be, that we've farmed out our responsibilities, especially for the disabled, to the state—and I'm grateful to Santorum for forcing on me the discomfort of having to think about the moral implications of his daughter's smile.[2]

Bella has opened our eyes to many things: the importance of treasuring each day, how to hope even in the darkest of circumstances, that faith is our foundation, and most important, what pure, unselfish love looks like. As we look back on another year of life, another year of miracles, we are filled with gratitude and hope. We are grateful for one more year of life with our precious girl. We are hopeful that through the witness of Bella's spirit, people will continue to be inspired, challenged to think about the "moral implications" of my daughter's smile. Through her life, we see that value is not determined by what society calls "usefulness," but, rather, value is measured by our capacity to love.

17

LOVE GIVES
PURPOSE

• *Rick Santorum* •

*God is looking for people through whom he can
do the impossible. What a pity we plan to do
only the things that we can do ourselves.*

—A. W. TOZER

One of Bella's gifts is that she has no plans to do anything for herself. She seems perfectly happy being able to do almost nothing for herself. She can't wash herself, dress herself, stand on her own, crawl, walk, feed herself, or tell us how she feels or where it hurts. She will always need our care.

None of this appears to distress her. She doesn't get frustrated by any of her apparent deficiencies. She is just content to be who she is. Now, medical experts may opine that she lacks the mental capacity to feel otherwise. I am fairly certain that if such a statement were made, it would be wrong. Bella does at times get upset, irritable, and even demanding. She does so for the same reasons you and I would express those emotions. Unlike with many of my less-than-pleasant moments, however, when the demand is met, the lack of sleep or the pain goes away, so does her complaint.

During my presidential run, the country got to know of Bella. They learned of her illness in February that caused me to suspend the campaign within days after I was announced, belatedly, the winner of the Iowa caucuses. Because of her illness and its impact on our campaign, we felt compelled to release information about Bella's condition, Trisomy 18, and all the physical complications that made her illness more serious.

That is what they knew of Bella, but the country had no way of knowing any of the things about who she is—her personality, likes, and dislikes. Out of an excess of caution because of the way the media and the left treated Sarah Palin's son, Trig, with Trisomy 21, we kept all our comments about Bella to her condition, not her physical and cognitive abilities. In fact, the only insight anyone could have gleaned from the information we provided about Bella was a picture we released to the press and on our website of Bella sitting on her daddy's lap on the front porch of our house. That picture of an adorable smiling little girl with her completely enthralled daddy was the only glimpse the country had of who she really is.

As Karen and I sat in her room in January 2012, enduring Bella's first hospitalization in more than two years, it really never crossed our minds what was going on outside of that room. We were obviously completely focused on Bella's minute-by-minute condition, but there was also part of me that felt maybe God was pulling me out of the intensity of the race to give me perspective.

This race, even though we had only had three primaries so far, had been going on intensely for almost a year, and Bella's illness was only one of the considerations. Over the past few weeks, Karen and I had had some very candid conversations about all the children, not to mention how she was holding up. Most of the kids were doing fine. In fact, some of them were really blossoming. The cool factor of having a dad run for president was wearing thin, however, as the reality of having both more responsibilities at home and unwanted attention at school and on social media began to sink in. At Bella's bedside, I looked at the face of a mom who had been up all night and stretched as thin as plastic wrap over a container, holding everything in place. Even though we had just been declared the winner in Iowa (two and a half weeks after the caucus), I had to broach the subject of getting out of the race. Her response took me aback.

Karen was the last of our family to sign off on getting in the race. When I started traveling to Iowa, New Hampshire, and South Carolina in 2010, the press began asking questions about running for president. I recall our first serious conversation about the idea of running. I talked about all the reasons I was thinking of running. Why I was feeling called to run. After I finished, Karen's answer was right to the point. "No."

I said, "Fine. I think we both need to pray about it before we decide anything."

She said, "No."

I said, "Honey, you and I always have prayed about decisions like this." In fact, Karen is a big-time prayer warrior and never makes any decision of consequence without taking it to God in prayer.

She fired back, "God could not possibly want you to run for president!" Then she proceeded to lay out a list of reasons why God had to agree with her.

When she finished, I said, "I'll put you in the undecided category for now!"

Over the next few months, Karen slowly, but surely, came to the same mind as mine. In fact, she admitted that while she didn't want me to run, she had felt God's call on her heart from the very beginning. She simply didn't want to take on that cross, at least not at that time in our lives.

As we sat next to Bella's bedside, thinking we were going to be in the hospital for days or even weeks, I couldn't help but think that, though Bella was the principal impetus for me to get into the race, it now looked as though she might be the trigger for my exit. I couldn't imagine leaving her side. I sometimes tease Karen and the children that Bella loves me the most, but they know Bella and I have that special daddy–little girl bond. She loves to play with Daddy throwing her up in the air, spin dancing, and doing "Bell-ups," lifting her above my head so she can touch the ceiling. We have our quiet time, too, where Bella's innocence and unfiltered joy pulls me in. There was no way I was going anywhere until she was out of the woods, and the last time she was in this condition, she was on a ventilator for five weeks in the intensive care unit.

When I broached the subject with Karen, I thought she would simply say, "It's over." Instead she made many wise observations about both our campaign and personal lives but concluded with "Bella will tell us what is in store for us."

Karen was right. When the doctor came in moments later with the news on Bella's chest X-ray, it appeared Bella had spoken. It was awful. Her lungs were full of fluid. They looked just like the previous pneumonia.

After the initial shock, Karen looked at me and said, "We just need to pray for a miracle. Bella's life is a daily miracle, so today we just have a more immediate request."

And pray we did, all day and into the night, but we were not alone. We kept getting texts and e-mails from all over about people praying for Bella, including her special friend Brendan Kelly. We could feel the power of the intercessory prayers, and there was no doubt that so could Bella. Nights are always worse than her days, so we hunkered down for the worst.

The next morning brought the X-ray tech to take a new chest X-ray to compare with the day before. We were hoping for stability; no worse than the day before. They weren't only stable; her lungs were perfectly clear. All the fluid was gone! For a normal person such a turnaround is highly improbable; for a lung-compromised Trisomy 18 child, well, Bella told us what was in store for us.

Throughout the night she had required less, not more, oxygen support, and that continued through the day. Bella was going to be moved out of intensive care to a step-down unit.

Now what to do? Karen and I decided to look at this respite

as a chance for the two of us to spend quiet time with each other in prayer, see the Lord at work, and try to make some sense of what this all meant for our family and the campaign.

We made a strategic decision that we would have never made but for Bella's illness. We decided not to go back to Florida for the last few days before the primary, but to jump ahead to three states that were having caucuses the week after the Nevada primary. We would get a jump on our competitors and have more time to run the kind of grassroots, personal campaign that led to our success in Iowa.

Bella was doing so well we decided on Sunday morning to travel to suburban Missouri, St. Charles County, on Monday, and restart the campaign the very next afternoon. I must admit, I questioned the wisdom of scheduling our "restart" campaign event with only twenty-four hours' notice to a state where I had not done much campaigning. Because I wanted to talk about providing training for jobs that would be created with our manufacturing plan, we planned on holding the event at the logical place for that training—a community college. To say the least, colleges are not a hotbed of support for any conservative presidential candidate; we wouldn't have a built-in crowd on such short notice.

By Monday morning, Bella was back to being all smiles, so I was off to Missouri. I knew the media was going to cover my return to the trail and was concerned that the expected small crowd would result in a snarky headline, like "Santorum returns, nobody notices." When we pulled up to the auditorium on campus, I panicked. There was a good, not great, crowd, but they were standing outside the building. All I could think was that we couldn't get in touch with the college over the weekend and never booked the auditorium. When I got out of the car, I was greeted by our lead staffer at the event, and I told him to open the doors and let the people in. He told me the auditorium was packed with several hundred people, and this was the *overflow*.

There was an energy and enthusiasm I had not seen since we were in Iowa a month before. What was happening? As I took the stage amid a frenzy of enthusiasm, three people caught my eye. Right in the front row was a young man in a wheelchair. I am sure we had people in wheelchairs at other campaign events, but the expression on his face grabbed me. For a flash there was no one else in the room as he mouthed the words *thank you*.

I then swung to my left to wave to the crowd, and there stood a tall young man with a five- or six-year-old child on his shoulders, waving a sign back and forth. The little girl had Down syndrome, Trisomy 21. The sign read, "I'm for Bella's Dad!"

From that point on in the campaign, they came—to rallies, to volunteer, to social media, and anywhere else to be part of a campaign that valued people equally. A few weeks later I met a young man with spina bifida in Oklahoma City. Our whole team was excited to meet him. He had completed more advocacy and get-out-the-vote calls in the last two months than anyone else in the country—from his home, in his wheelchair.

For the rest of the campaign, from shaking hands with rally goers at rope lines, to checking in to another hotel, the first thing out of most people's mouths after hello was, "How is your daughter?" or just "How's Bella?" It continued after the campaign for months. Even now, most days someone I don't know asks me about Bella.

I have never asked, but I suspect from comments I have

received since the campaign that many people saw her as the underdog beating the odds, and Americans love an underdog. Others saw a family with its priorities in the right place—family first, even if it means backing out of a presidential race. Neither of these points of view were limited to Democrats or Republicans or liberals or conservatives. Just a few days after I announced my withdrawal from the campaign, Elizabeth, Sarah Maria, and I attended the White House Correspondents' Dinner. (I didn't want to go, but the girls said it was payback for dragging them all over the country.) I felt like a paparazzo taking pictures of them with all the Hollywood celebrities in attendance. After the click, most of the stars, from George Clooney to Sofía Vergara, asked how Bella was and said something like this: "I don't agree with your politics, but I was impressed with how hard you worked in your campaign and how you put your family first."

At the root of that statement is the recognition that a mentally and physically challenged little girl who counts every day on earth as a miracle is worth it. This was coming from many people who would think nothing of aborting a child with Bella's condition. That only makes sense if they look at Bella and children like her not through their own eyes, but through the eyes of a father who loved her. It allowed them to see her not as a personal inconvenience, as a burden to society, or as having no economic utility, but for who she is: a beautiful soul.

Love opens up windows not only for the lover but also for those who see love in action. Bella is a font of love from which all our family drinks every day and who, through God's perfect plan, opened the eyes of a confused and misguided world to see the truth that only love can reveal.

18

LOVE BRINGS HOPE

• Karen Santorum •

*Hope does not disappoint us, because God's
love has been poured into our hearts through
the Holy Spirit who has been given to us.*

—ROMANS 5:5

A s Rick and I conclude this book, we are overwhelmed with gratitude. The Lord has blessed us with so much. It is the gift of living faith, however, that has opened our eyes to see His love in a special way in the eyes of our little angel, Bella. We tell Bella's story so that her sufferings and strength may remind people of where real hope comes from: our Lord Jesus Christ. Our friend, and world-renowned evangelist, Nick Vujicic, who was born without arms and legs and lives a successful and blessed life, expressed this eloquently:

> God loves you and he hasn't forgotten your pain. He hasn't forgotten your family. And maybe as you're watching this interview, you've compared your suffering to my suffering. And that's not where hope is, to know that someone else, in your opinion, is suffering more than you. That's not where hope is. The hope is in the name of God; the name of the Lord Jesus Christ. Hope is when you compare your suffering to the infinite, immeasurable love and grace of God. Isaiah 40:31 says those who wait upon the Lord will renew their strength and they shall mount up on wings as eagles. I didn't need my circumstances to change. I don't need arms and legs. I need the wings of the Holy Spirit, and I'm flying because I know Jesus is holding me up. Don't give up on God, because God will not give up on you.[1]

Many doctors warned us that Bella's condition would mean total dependency and full-time care. Thus, we anticipated the daily demands of her care, the late nights waking to beeping alarms, and her vulnerable immune system. These are the biological, material realities of her condition. She relies completely on us for food, shelter, care, and love. Dependency. Helplessness. Yet, in the same way, isn't that how God must see us? We are the lost, wandering lambs from the fold, who depend completely on their Shepherd for life, mercy, and redemption.

Infinitely more broken and dependent than Bella, ours is a spiritual, not a physical, weakness. We're more dependent than Bella, because we *have* more and therefore *want* more and feel pain, distress, and anxiety when we lose something or don't get what we think we need or want.

All Bella knows, in her total dependency, is the *love* that surrounds her and sustains her every moment of every day. And what is the fruit of her total dependency and her being sustained by love? It is her love that radiates every moment of every day. The essence of her very being is loving everyone who comes into her world; we see it in the joy of her eyes, the breadth of her smile, the song of her giggle, and the squeeze of her hand. We can do nothing of any measure for Him, save loving Him. Bella teaches us that is enough. In fact, it is all that matters.

We burden and we lift burdens; it's all a part of being the body of Christ; it's all part of loving Christ more completely.

◆   ◆   ◆

As the Alzheimer's progressed for the last few years of my dear father's life, my extraordinary mother took care of him and attended to his every need. He was always clean, well dressed, properly nourished, and given the gift and peace of remaining at home. Our family was there every day for my mom, helping out in many ways. As the Alzheimer's stole my dad's brilliant mind, what remained were his sweet smiles, gentleness, and kindness. And even as the disease became more entrenched, Dad was never pushed aside or forgotten. We continued to talk to him and care for him. We still saw his dignity.

In my parents' sixty-seventh year of marriage, my father

died surrounded by his loving family and pastor. Rick and I were there at his side, holding his hand as my mother kissed his head and told him she would love him for all eternity. As my father hovered in the veil between heaven and earth, the last words he heard from his family were those of gratitude and love.

My mother's sacrificial love and constant devotion to my father were a powerful witness to our family. She lived out her marital vows with love, until the very end, and reminded us that Christ teaches that we are here to serve others. "More than that, we rejoice in our sufferings, knowing that suffering produces endurance, and endurance produces character, and character produces hope, and hope does not disappoint us, because God's love has been poured into our hearts through the Holy Spirit who has been given to us" (Rom. 5:3–5).

Rick and I will be forever grateful to my mother for inspiring us to emulate and live that sort of love. We know without a doubt that her strength and example during my upbringing, throughout our marriage, and particularly as she cared for my father, in turn gave us the strength to navigate life with Bella.

As we reflect back on the days that followed Bella's birth, we now realize the peace Rick was feeling came from Christ's love. It was God's way of strengthening him so he could hold our family together as the storm thrust shards of glass into our hearts. He experienced peace within the storm, and that kind of peace only comes from complete trust and hope in Christ.

For whatever was written in former days was written for our instruction, that by steadfastness and by the encouragement of the scriptures we might have hope. May the God of

steadfastness and encouragement grant you to live in such
harmony with one another, in accord with Christ Jesus, that
together you may with one voice glorify the God and Father
of our Lord Jesus Christ. (Rom. 15:4–6)

No one escapes suffering. Everyone goes through tough times. Suffering is a part of our human condition and cannot be avoided. Setbacks, failures, pain, suffering, and hardships are all a part of life, but whether we are able to find peace within the storm depends on our resilience and perseverance. Whenever one of our children tells us that they don't want to fail at something, we remind them that there will be times in their life when they *will* fail, but it's how they come through it that matters. If we choose to focus on the negative, the failure itself, the darkness will oppress and consume us. Eventually it will destroy a person. We need to embrace the fact that we're human and our lives will be filled with suffering and hardship, but we have the ultimate hope and victory in Our Lord.

As we cared for Bella daily in the NICU, it was a dark time for me. I was allowing despair to consume and exhaust me. I did not have peace in the midst of the storm. Eventually, however, I realized that, as during the birthing of a baby, I needed to embrace the pain. I needed to feel the pain more fully so that I could move through it and allow it to strengthen me. I was walking through fire. And like iron being forged in the fire, or brass polished by friction, that time in the desert shaped me and helped me to grow.

As I found my joy again and reclaimed my hope, I knew that I needed to forgive the doctors, critics, and skeptics who did not want to give Bella a chance. I prayed for their change of heart and I prayed for the grace to forgive them as the Scripture says, "Let all bitterness and wrath and anger and clamor and slander be put away from you, with all malice, and be kind to one another, tenderhearted, forgiving one another, as God in Christ forgave you" (Eph. 4:31–32). I understand that everyone makes mistakes, and we've all said and done things that we wish we could take back. As time went on, I stopped dwelling on whether their actions were out of ignorance or malice. Through God's grace, my heart healed from their wounds. I forgave them and carry no bitterness or wrath. My only hope is that maybe the naysayers will pick up this book someday and realize what the world would have missed without Bella and others like her.

How did we crawl out of a pit of despair and maintain a sense of hope? Our help came from a lot of prayers and a book, *Arise from Darkness*, by Fr. Benedict J. Groeschel. We had read it many years before and realized during Bella's first year of life that we needed to read it again. Our life was like a pendulum swinging between joy and desperation. The book reminded us of precious truths that we knew but had forgotten in the stress of the time. Father Groeschel's book reminded us to use suffering and hardship as a time for spiritual growth and healing. He instructs us to see the joy we receive when we place our hope and trust in God and truly, completely live them in our daily lives.

He also pointed out another essential life skill—to lighten up. We need to laugh more at ourselves. We need to feel joy more consistently. So after bringing Bella home from the NICU, or the PICU, Rick and I would make sure to have fun as a family. We did things we had always done, but needed to do again. We went for hikes, swung on our tree swing, played board games, and watched *I Love Lucy* reruns. Rick took the kids on tractor rides, and we rejoiced in a thousand other happy ways to maintain the joy in our home. This helped our family immensely, especially during Bella's first few years of life during the times when we felt knocked down, only to get kicked again. Our experience proved to us that hope keeps us going, it gives us joy, and it reminds us that things will get better if we accept our suffering and trust in God's love, knowing He is there, helping us to bear our cross.

I'll never forget one of my instructors in nursing school telling the class, "When patients lose hope, they die." She explained that hope keeps us moving forward and gives us the fortitude and encouragement to overcome whatever obstacles or pain we may be experiencing. She went on to explain that one of our roles as nurses is to help our patients to have hope—not false hope, but hope in something, anything good. During my orientation as a NICU nurse, the head nurse also stressed the importance of sharing the positive aspects of a baby's condition when giving parents an update on the baby's plan of care. She said that the babies feel their parents' love and hope.

When Bella was six months old and in the hospital, I remember sitting at her bedside, holding her tiny hands, and sobbing. I had been praying fervently, but could find nothing good in her situation. I then did what I always do in times of distress: I called my dear mother. She calmed me and reminded me that there are blessings even in the worst situations. She told me to go around the room and give thanks to God for all the blessings.

Perplexed, and a little taken aback, I hesitated, then did

what she had asked. It took a while, but eventually I realized that the tubes and machines I had been resenting were actually immense blessings. They were sustaining my little girl and helping her to heal. When we're able to see the blessings in every situation, as hard as it may be, it elevates us to another level, and we feel gratitude, followed by joy. This is not always easy to do, and it is something I need to keep reminding myself of during each new challenge.

We thank God every day for Bella. She has taught us that hope in Christ brings joy. We don't know where our lives would be without her. We look at her every day and see the face of God. We know that this little girl, who some misguided doctors thought would be such a burden, has actually become one of our greatest blessings. Bella has shown us that every life is a gift. Bella is totally dependent and totally at peace with her dependence. All that she doesn't have doesn't matter. As Nick Vujicic suggests, she doesn't need her circumstances to change; she has all that she needs. Bella, in her total dependency, lives only to love and to be loved. It's all she knows and all she needs. Her "infirmities" are what free her completely and give her peace and joy as she soars on eagles' wings.

Bella has taught us all how to live. We have come to realize our own infirmities, all that we "lack" or complain or worry about. We have come to realize our complete dependency. We have learned what really, what only, matters. God has given us the gift of Bella because He wants us all to be like Bella. If we recognize His all-encompassing, all-sustaining love, we will forget our infirmities and do what Bella does—love everyone in our world, experience the peace that passes understanding, and radiate pure joy.

Through Bella, God gives us the grace to cooperate with His will and empty ourselves for others. Then we can become His arms, embracing the world; His legs, still walking dusty streets; and His heart, still beating with the Divine Compassion manifested in Jesus Christ, the One who became the least of these in order to bring all of us into the full communion of Love.

We hoped. We hoped in Christ, and He allowed His divine grace to shine within us during the darkest times.

Our little Bella has taught us so much about the way to walk along on this path of life. Through her, we are learning more about how to love and finding hope that never disappoints. She teaches us more every day. She fills us with heavenly hope, the kind that reaches out and shines its light into every area of life. We hope that by reading about her, she will touch you as well, no matter where you are in your journey.

A MOTHER'S
NOTE OF
ENCOURAGEMENT

• Karen Santorum •

G od bless you, for you have been thrown into an unknown world, an emotional storm, and a sea of confusion. It's extremely painful and exhausting, but know that you are stronger than you think. I promise you things *will* get better. Where there is grief there is also healing.

Your child has a place in your family and in your hearts. Give him or her a name and honor the dignity of his or her life. You will never regret *love*! Take a lot of pictures and videos. Create keepsakes, such as, footprints and handprints in either ink or plaster of Paris, save locks of hair, blankets and clothing, or ID bracelets. It will be hard, but I promise you it *will* get better.

Love your husbands completely and unconditionally, and understand that you will grieve differently and that's all right. Remember the beauty and meaning of marital love. Make your world simpler so that your other children will also receive your love and time. It will be hard, but I promise you it *will* get better.

Take one day, one step at a time, and realize that you can't do it all. Allow people to love you by helping with meals, the children, the house, and giving you some time to breathe. Find comfort in support groups.

"Always seek to do good to one another and to all. Rejoice always, pray constantly, give thanks in all circumstances; for this is the will of God in Christ Jesus for you" (1 Thess. 5:11–18). Use your faith to strengthen you. You can't do it, but God always can. He loves you so much!

When you are at the end of your life standing before God, the only thing that will matter is how much you *loved*.

A FATHER'S
NOTE OF
ENCOURAGEMENT

• Rick Santorum •

I t's true that "God doesn't give us more than we can handle," but that doesn't mean we won't be stretched thin and at times broken in the process. Place all your trust in God and lean on Him. Pray fervently. One of my favorites is "The Universal Prayer": "Lord, I believe in Thee; may I believe more strongly. I trust in Thee; may I hope more confidently. I love Thee; may I love Thee more ardently . . . May I learn from Thee the nothingness of this world, the greatness of heaven, the shortness of time, and the length of eternity." Your child will help you to grow in love and holiness. You just have to allow it. You *will* come through the dark valley and into the light.

The most important thing, besides our faith, in caring for a child with disabilities is a strong marriage. Pay attention to your marriage, nurture it, and dive all in. Love your wife completely and unconditionally and understand that there is no room for selfishness in marriage. To the people who think happiness can be found someplace else—you are dead wrong—just look through your photo albums.

Esto vir! This means "be a man" in Latin. Real men don't abandon their wives and children—especially when they need you the most. It's true, your life has changed and you'll never be the same. It's painful and it's hard, but it's also an opportunity to grow in character. Fathers are the protectors of their families. Real men don't walk away from a good fight, and it's your wife, precious child, and family that you're fighting for now. *Esto vir!*

ACKNOWLEDGMENTS

First and foremost, Rick and I thank our dear Lord for all His tremendous blessings in our lives. "O give thanks to the Lord, for he is good; his steadfast love endures forever (Ps. 18:1)! The greatest blessings being our marriage and each and every one of our children: Elizabeth, John, Daniel, Sarah Maria, Peter, Patrick, and Bella. Thank you dear daughters and sons of ours for all your love, support, and patience as we were writing this book. You are all loved "to the moon . . . and back!"

Rick and I give special thanks to our daughter Elizabeth, who cowrote *Bella's Gift* with us. It was a complete joy working on this project with you, precious Elizabeth! We laughed, we cried, and shared our hearts with each other. Thank you for your insights, beautifully expressed thoughts, hard work, and organization. Thank you for keeping your procrastinating and busy parents on schedule. *Bella's Gift* is a very special book because of you. We love you so much, darling!

As always, my dear mother was a great inspiration and pillar of strength throughout the writing and various stages of this book. Anytime I was overwhelmed or completely emotional as I was writing, Mom, you always calmed my anxious heart. Thank you for all your love, encouragement, and wisdom. You are such a huge blessing to our family. We love you beyond words!

Huge thanks from the bottom of our hearts to Bridget O'Donnell who was an answer to our prayers many years ago. This book would not have been possible if not for your exceptional help and care of our family, especially our sweet little Bella. You have walked every single step of this journey with us and we're so grateful for all your love and kindness through the years. As you know, my entire family loves you, Bridget!

Rick and I thank our dear friends Mark and Leanne Rodgers, who have traveled an amazing journey with us for the past twenty-five years. We've worked on so many issues and projects together, gone to more dinners and trips than we care to count. It's been so much fun sharing all our hearts and lives with both of you. Thank you, Mark, for being a great book agent and thank you both for editing the book. Your recommendations improved the book. We feel immense love and gratitude toward you.

We thank Nadine Maenza, the executive director of our political action committee, Patriot Voices, and a dear friend for the past twenty years. Nadine is also someone who, like us, experienced the death of a child and has raised a child with a disability. Nadine, you get it and you've always understood us. Your empathy and kindness have been great blessings to us. We also give huge heartfelt thanks to our steadfast friend John Brabender. For the past twenty-five years you've used your brilliant gifts to let the people of Pennsylvania and the rest of the country get to know us. You are amazing, John, and we treasure your friendship. Thank you, Nadine, John, and our fantastic communications director, Virginia Davis, for editing the book and for everything you're doing to make sure *Bella's Gift* will touch many hearts and lives.

We cannot thank our editor, Janene MacIvor, enough for all her guidance and thoughtfulness with *Bella's Gift*. Janene, you always provided valuable advice and direction and did it with so much joy! Thank you for your encouragement every step of the way and for sharing our happiness every time we reached a milestone. In addition to Janene, Rick and I are extremely grateful to the entire team at Thomas Nelson Publishing who helped with *Bella's Gift*: publisher, Brian Hampton; marketing VP, Chad Cannon; marketing managers, Erica Reid and Katy Boatman; publicity, Emily Lineberger; packaging design, Belinda Bass; and graphic designer, Walter Petrie. Thank you all for your exceptional work on *Bella's Gift*.

We give many thanks to our friends Deacon Keith Fournier and Sharon Hickson. You were so generous with your time, suggestions, and edits. It touched our hearts that you cared deeply about this project. Deacon Keith, thank you for your love for Bella and your spiritual guidance that strengthens us. We cherish your friendship. We also thank our family friend Steven Munoz, who lost a lot of sleep working on the pictures with us! You are a whiz on the computer and the pictures would never have been on time without you. Thank you, also, Steven for always being there for our family. You are a true and loved friend to every member of our clan.

Thank you to Ben Kafferlin for your support and for getting the copyright permission for the story "Welcome to Holland" by Emily Perl Kingsley. Thank you, Emily, for allowing us to use your wonderful story that perfectly sums up a parent's feelings.

Words cannot begin to express how much fun we've had when Liz Zernich has taken our children's pictures. We've been going to the Timeless Portraits by Liz studio in Sewickley, Pennsylvania, for twenty years and have enjoyed every minute of being in such a delightful and cheerful place. Thank you, Liz, for taking the most beautiful pictures of Bella and for giving us the gifts of capturing joyful memories that we will treasure forever. You are so kind and talented, and we can't wait to have Bella visit the moon, the English garden, and the castle just as her brothers and sisters did!

Notes

Chapter 1
1. *Our Sunday Visitor's Catholic Encyclopedia.*

Chapter 1
1. Sirach 6:14.

Chapter 3
1. Rick Santorum, from his speech at the Republican National Convention, Tampa, FL, August 28, 2012.

Chapter 5
1. Avelino de Almeida, in John De Marchi, *The Immaculate Heart, The True Story of Our Lady of Fátima* (New York: Farrar, Straus and Young, 1952), 144.

Chapter 10

1. Written in 1534, while Thomas More was in the Tower of London, awaiting execution. You can find this passage in Thomas More's *The Sadness of Christ*, edited by Gerard Wegemer, Yale University Press translation (New Rochelle, NY: Scepter, 1997), 142.

Chapter 15

1. Jean Vanier, *From Brokenness to Community* (Mahwah, NJ: Paulist Press, 1992), 26–28. Mr. Vanier, a theologian and humanitarian, is the founder of L'Arche, an international network of communities for the intellectually disabled.

Chapter 16

1. "Apostolic Journey of Pope Benedict XVI to Portugal on the Occasion of the Tenth Anniversary of the Beatification of Jacinta and Francisco, Young Shepherds of Fátima: Meeting with the World of Culture: Address of His Holiness Benedict XVI," May 12, 2010, transcript, on the website of Libreria Editrice Vaticana, http://www.vatican.va/holy_father/benedict_xvi/speeches/2010/may/documents/hf_ben-xvi_spe_20100512_incontro-cultura_en.html.
2. Joe Klein, "Rick Santorum's Inconvenient Truths," *Time*, March 5, 2012.

Chapter 18

1. Nick Vujicic, "Unstoppable," *700 Club* Interactive, CBN, March 20, 2013, http://www.cbn.com/tv/2239031407001.

NAMES AND CAPTIONS FOR *PHOTO INSERT*

Page 1:

Bella—Our Beautiful Angel on Earth!
Photo courtesy of "Timeless Portraits by Liz," Sewickley, PA

Page 2:

Top row, left to right: Bella's Baptism (left to right: John, Sarah
Maria, Rick, Patrick, Father Alexander Drummond, Bella in her
isolette, Daniel, Peter, and Elizabeth); Grandma and Granddad
Garver with Bella
Second row, left to right: our first family picture with Bella
(standing, left to right: Daniel, John, Rick, and Elizabeth; sitting,
left to right: Peter, Patrick, Karen (holding Bella) and Sarah
Maria); big sister and godmother Elizabeth

Third row, left to right: Nana and PopPop Santorum holding Bella; our friend Susie Twetten holding Bella

Page 3:

Top row, left to right: Patrick and Bella; Peter and Bella; Karen holding Bella, our friend Katy Ryland and Rick at Bella's first birthday party

Bella's first birthday party with family friends (left to right: Chris and Lee Goodwin, Walt and Susie Twetten. Rick, Bella, Karen, John, Mary Ferguson, Gary and Jennifer Hale, Peter, Sarah Maria, Elizabeth, Patrick, and Daniel)

Page 4:

Top row, left to right: Bella with Karen on her first birthday; Bella playing cards with her big brothers Peter and Patrick

Middle picture: loving big sister Sarah Maria reading a book to Bella

Bottom row, left to right: Sarah Maria, Peter, and Patrick playing with Bella; Bella in her swing; Bella sitting in her chair as the kids see how cute she looks in hats

Page 5:

Bella in her flowers and lace hat looking adorable!

Photo courtesy of "Timeless Portraits by Liz," Sewickley, PA

Page 6:

Top row, left to right: Sarah Maria holding Bella, Patrick, and Peter welcome Bella home from the hospital; proud big brother John experiencing the joy of holding Bella; Bella's special friend Brendan Kelly with Bella

Bottom picture: Bella celebrated her first Christmas! (Elizabeth holding Bella, Sarah Maria, Peter, Patrick, Daniel, and John)

Page 7:

Bella is loved by her aunts, uncles, and cousins!

Top row, left to right: Bella's cousin Emily (holding Bella) and her husband James Dudt; Bella's aunt Kathy Lamb holding Bella

Center: Bella's uncle Bill and aunt Nancy Garver holding Bella

Bottom row, left to right: Bella's uncle Dan Santorum with Bella; Bella's cousin Olivia Garver and Bella; Bella's aunt Sis (Marybeth Kusturiss) with Bella

Page 8:

Bella is loved by her aunts, uncles, and cousins!

Top row, left to right: Bella's cousin Fran (holding Bella) and her husband Joe Urmann; Bella's uncle Paul (holding Bella) and Bella's aunt Carolyn Garver

Middle row, left to right: Bella's cousin Lee Garver, uncle Ken Garver, cousin Jessica Berkey (holding Bella), and aunt Marsha Garver; Bella's aunt Maureen Swartz with Bella

Third row: Aunt Anna Estop-Garver and Uncle Jim Garver holding Bella

Bottom row, left to right: Bella's uncle Bob Garver and Bella; Bella's cousins Jessica Berkey and Matt Garver holding Bella

Page 9:

Bella loves having fun!

Bella looking too cute!

Our angel Bella

Bella having a tea party with bear

Photos courtesy of "Timeless Portraits by Liz," Sewickley, PA

Page 10:

Top row, left to right: Bella's third birthday party (left to right: Patrick, John, Peter, Elizabeth, Sarah Maria, Daniel, and Bella); proud big brother Daniel

Middle row, left to right: proud daddy and Bella; Christmas 2010 (top row, left to right: Elizabeth, Rick, Bella, Karen, John; bottom row, left to right: Daniel, Peter, Patrick, and Sarah Maria)

Bottom left: a special fresco of our angel Bella was painted by artists Roger and Karen Nitz for the Bella Donna Chapel in McKinney, Texas. Our friends, Jeff and Donna Blackard, who own the chapel commissioned the painting.

Page 11:

Top row, left to right: Bella taking a walk with Sarah Maria, Peter, Karen, and Daniel; Bella taking a bike ride with Patrick, Rick, Karen, and Peter

Middle row, left to right: Bella fishing with the boys (left to right: Rick, Patrick, Bella, Daniel, and Peter; Bella swimming with Patrick, Peter, and Rick

Bottom row, left to right: Bella at the beach with Rick; Bella playing piano with Elizabeth; Bella enjoying a tractor ride; Bella reading a book with Patrick

Page 12:

Top row, left to right: John and Bella, Bella's babysitter/nurse and family friend Bridget O'Donnell holding Bella

Middle row, left to right: Our family at the beach (standing, left to right: friend Steven Munoz, Patrick, John, Daniel, Peter, Elizabeth, Sarah Maria, and friend Bridget O'Donnell; sitting, left to right: Grandma Garver, Rick, Bella, and Karen); Elizabeth and Bella, Sarah Maria and Bella

Bottom row, left to right: Bella's fifth birthday (standing, left to right: Patrick, John, Karen, Daniel, Sarah Maria; Peter is kneeling with Bella on his shoulders; Elizabeth was away at college); our friends Leanne and Mark Rodgers (holding Bella). Mark is Bella's godfather.

Page 13:

Bella is loved by so many friends!

First row, left to right: Father Julio Rivero and Bella; Tommy Johnson with Bella; Annie Ryland with Bella; Frank Hanna with Bella

Second row, left to right: Mary Katherine and Ellie Twetten and Bella; Father Jerome Fasano and Bella; our builder and family friend Anders Hurd (holding Bella) and assistant Jared Willard (Anders built Bella's disability bedroom, bathroom, therapy room, and ramps); Anna Fronzaglia with Bella

Third row, left to right: Jennifer Morano (holding Bella) and Father Julio Rivero; Mark, Peter, and Muriel Forrest holding Bella; Ercy and Senora Maria Rodriguez and Bella

Fourth row, left to right: Foster and Lynn Friess (holding Bella); Mark and Katy Ryland with Bella

Bottom row, left to right: Frank, Maura, and Brendan Kelly (holding Bella), Karen and Rick; Donna Blackard and Bella; Father John Mosimann holding Bella

Page 14:

Some of Bella's Exceptional Caregivers

Top row, left to right: Bella's nutritionist Robin Cook; Bella's physical therapist Francie Mitchell; Bella's pediatrician Dr. James Baugh

Middle row, left to right: Bella's surgeon Dr. Thane Blinman; Bella's physical therapist Francie Mitchell

Bottom row: upper and lower left is Bella's occupational therapist Lynne Ganz; one of Bella's pulmonologists Dr. Sunil Kapoor; Bella's registered nurse Erin MacEgan

Page 15:

Top row, left to right: Grandma and Granddad Garver with Bella; standing, left to right: Peter, Daniel, Bella, Elizabeth, Nana Santorum, Sarah Maria, John, Patrick, and PopPop Santorum is sitting

Bottom picture: our family on vacation with Grandma Garver (standing, left to right: Daniel, John, Grandma Garver, Peter, and Patrick; sitting, left to right: Sarah Maria, Rick, Bella, Karen, and Elizabeth)

Page 16:

Sugar and Spice and Everything Nice
That's What Little Bella Is Made Of
Photo courtesy of "Timeless Portraits by Liz," Sewickley, PA

ABOUT THE
AUTHORS

Karen Santorum, one of twelve children and a former neonatal intensive care nurse and attorney, received a bachelor of science in nursing from Duquesne University in Pittsburgh, Pennsylvania, and worked for several years in a Neonatal Intensive Care Unit. Her juris doctorate degree is from the University of Pittsburgh School of Law where she was a Law Review member. Karen is the author of two books, *Letters to Gabriel* and *Everyday Graces: A Child's Book of Good Manners*. Karen and her husband of almost twenty-five years, Rick, are the parents of eight children: Elizabeth, John, Daniel,

Gabriel, Sarah Maria, Peter, Patrick, and Isabella. Her greatest role and love in life is being a full-time mother at home. According to Karen, "There is no greater joy in life than to be a mother. It is the most important job I will ever have."

◆ ◆ ◆

Rick Santorum, a native of Pennsylvania, was a candidate for the Republican nomination for president of the United States in 2012. He served in the House of Representatives from 1991 to 1995 and in the Senate from 1995 to 2007 and is the author of several books, including the 2005 *New York Times* bestseller *It Takes a Family*. Rick's most important role and love in life is being a husband and father.

◆ ◆ ◆

Elizabeth Santorum graduated *magna cum laude* from the University of Dallas. During the 2012 Republican presidential primary, she spent a year campaigning across the nation on behalf of her father, Senator Rick Santorum. Appearing on CNN, Fox News, NBC, and many other news outlets at twenty years old, she became one of the campaign's most requested speakers. Elizabeth has spent time doing mission work in Uganda, is currently a John Jay Fellow, and has always been a great big sister.